BX2170.C55 C33613 1993

Robert Webber

Institute for Worship Studies
Florida Campus

10000005178

D1801947

FROM THE LIBRARY OF
THE INSTITUTE FOR
WORSHIP STUDIES
FLORIDA CAMPUS

Odo Casel

The Mystery of Christ Made Present

Selected texts for the Christian Year

In association with the
Abbot Herwegen Institute
of the Abbey of Maria Laach

edited and introduced by
Arno Schilson

translated by Ronald Walls

ST. BEDE'S PUBLICATIONS
Petersham, Massachusetts

St. Bede's Publications
271 North Main Street
PO Box 545
Petersham, MA 01366-0545

The Mystery of Christ Made Present: Selected texts for the Christian Year is a translation of Gegenwart des Christus-Mysteriums: Ausgewählte Texte zum Kirchenjahr published in 1986 by Matthias-Grünewald-Verlag, Mainz, Germany.

This edition: Copyright © 1999 St. Bede's Publications

ALL RIGHTS RESERVED
PRINTED IN THE UNITED STATES OF AMERICA

LIBRARY OF CONGRESS CATALOGING-IN-PUBLICATION DATA

Casel, Odo, 1886-1948.
   [Gegenwart des Christus-Mysterium. English]
   The mystery of Christ made present: selected texts for the Christian year/Odo Casel; in association with the Abbot Herwegen Institute of the Abbey of Maria Laach edited and introduced by Arno Schilson; translated by Ronald Walls.
     p. cm.
   Includes bibliographical references (p.   ).
   ISBN 1-879007-38-X (paperback
    1. Church year meditations. 2. Christian life—Catholic authors.
   I. Schilson, Arno, 1945-   . II. Abt-Herwegen-Institut. III. Title.
BX2170.C55C33613   1999
242'.3—dc21   99-12918
                                                                           CIP

Contents

Foreword vii
Introduction ix

1. **Making Present the Mystery of Christ**
   The meaning of the Christian Year 1
2. **Advent**
   The life-style of a Christian 8
3. **Christmas**
   The Mystery of the Incarnation 20
4. **Christmastide**
   The crib and the cross 28
5. **The Epiphany of our Lord**
   Jesus, our way to God 35
6. **Good Friday**
   Authentic adoration of the cross 42
7. **Easter**
   The Lord's Pasch—passing over into new life 49
8. **The Easter Season**
   Pentecost—the symbol of completion 55
9. **The Ascension**
   The glorified Christ with cross in hand 62
10. **Pentecost**
    The Spirit—God gives himself to mankind 69
11. **The Assumption of Mary into Heaven**
    Abandonment to God is the way to life 77
12. **Peter and Paul**
    The meaning of devotion to the saints 84
Notes and references
   Notes and references 96
   Literature 99
   Bibliographies 100
   Life and works of Odo Casel—chronological table ... 101

Foreword

"THE MYSTERY OF CHRIST is always the same and always complete." These words of Odo Casel, whose hundredth birthday was celebrated on 27 September 1986, show, as do many other sayings of his, that his thought did not focus exclusively on the celebration of the Eucharist. The intention of this great stimulator amongst the theologians of our century was that his theology of divine worship should embrace the whole of the Christian's liturgical and sacramental life. His work on the eucharistic doctrine of St Justin Martyr was bound, therefore, to be applied also to other spheres of Christian life. Odo Casel did this very thoroughly. He was no mere scholar and specialist theologian, but a spiritual leader and guide for all enquiring men and women; and yet, in spite of his amazingly vast output, he had to restrict himself for the most part to the essays which still command our respect. His essays, expounding the whole of Christian life in terms of his fundamental view of the Mystery of Christ, are to be found mostly in the spiritual addresses which he gave regularly over a span of many years to the congregation of Benedictine nuns in the Abbey of the Holy Cross in Herstelle. Many of these, culled from notes and reviews, became accessible in literary form only after his premature death on Easter morning March 28, 1948. Odo Casel, however, certainly felt that the feasts of the Christian Year and their proper celebration urgently required theological and spiritual exposition.

Pursuing this aim, in 1941 he published a series of short works in a book entitled "The Christian Festival Mystery," from which Professor Dr. A. Schilson has taken most of the texts collected in this little volume. These are characteristic of Casel's personality, not only in their vivid display of his work as a scholar and theologian, but also in their equally clear revelation of his pastoral concern. Casel's desire was to proclaim and expound the Mystery of Christ to the faithful, but he wished also to lead them and accompany them on the way to that mystery. In these essays on the Christian Year he shows himself to be a true mystagogue in the sense in which he again and again applied this word to the Fathers of the Church whom he admired because of this characteristic.

The Abbot Herwegen Institute thanks Professor Schilson for his selection of the texts, and for his enlightening Introduction; and it thanks the Matthias-Grünewald-Verlag for their careful production of this new edition of Odo Casel.

Emmanuel V. Severus OSB
Maria Laach, the feast of St Justin Martyr, June 1, 1986.

Introduction

BOTH THE NAME and the highly developed mystical theology of the Benedictine monk Odo Casel (1886-1948) of the Abbey of Maria Laach in the Eifel are largely forgotten. So many of the stimuli, impulses and reforms, which are accepted today as our rightful heritage, are the product of his theological enterprise during the first half of the twentieth century; and yet scarcely anyone thinks of tracing them to their true origin, or of understanding them through reference to that origin. But the seismic liturgical and theological reform-movements in the Church during this century cannot properly be understood apart from the earlier, quiet but persistent work of Odo Casel. He was born into a generation that had lost all sense of perspective, at a time when the Church and theology were hesitant, helpless and often pulling in opposite directions; his outstanding achievement—like that of his contemporary Romano Guardini—was to point that generation along decisive paths. And so, from today's perspective, Odo Casel is to be valued as a theologian and reformer of the highest rank, and as a monitor and prophet for troubled times.

INTRODUCTION

I

Odo Casel provided a perspective and direction for an age, the spiritual, political, ecclesiastical and theological condition of which was desolate. The common view of the years after the turn of the century is that a change had taken place, thorough and deep enough to merit its being called a new epoch or a cultural revolution. The optimistic, forward-looking mood of the nineteenth century, the result of rapid technological and industrial development, had evaporated. Positivism and materialism as dominant intellectual tides, that is as comprehensive world-views, had lost their attraction. The much vaunted autonomy of the subject and the absolutizing of the individual at the expense of the community was suddenly transformed into a feeling of boundless loneliness and subjective threat. A mighty disenchantment was on the increase; resignation and disorientation followed.

There were signs of tentative fresh starts: philosophy of life made room for a sense of the unity of the world and its living, rational structures; the youth movement led to a new awareness of the essential value of community, and through its popularizing of hiking encouraged a feeling for nature; the law of form and objectivity in general were strictly observed, and mature values and accepted institutions were seen in a new and more favorable light; in addition there was a fumbling search for the transcendent, for mysticism, for the spiritual, for religion, for a mystery which of its nature is out of human reach.

Viewed politically, the first half of this century was no less shaken up by trends and events that led into new perspectives and a sense of hopelessness. After the loss of the First World War, Germany experienced a first collapse which was to have long-lasting effects. The end of the empire, the chaos of the Weimar Republic, the catastrophic economic situation, the Third Reich's misguided movement towards integration, with its almost unlimited potential for hope, which exploded at the end of the Second World War leaving a yawning chasm of resignation and despair—these were the political characteristics of the period in which Odo Casel, in his own fashion, contributed to a fundamental spiritual and theological renewal. The internal condition of the Church during this period was anything but hopeful. The attempt made by a few theologians at the turn of the century to read the signs of the times, and to give some space to historical thinking within the exposition of the truths of faith, was suppressed as modernism, and condemned with unexpected severity—a proceeding which seriously hampered and burdened Catholic theology until the time of the Second Vatican Council. A new age of restoration gained ground that was incapable of meeting the demands of the times. Instead, the groundswell of reform movements, above all the liturgical movement, the ecclesial movement and the Catholic youth movement constantly aroused mistrust on the part of Church leaders and were often groundlessly suspected and attacked. And so, every step in a new direction led to severe conflicts of conscience and very often to most severe ecclesiastical regulation.

Nonetheless a fresh mentality was slowly but persistently making headway within theological circles. Romano Guardini was already speaking of the re-awakening of the Church in people's souls. By this he meant that a purely external view of the Church as a social entity was giving way to a view of the Church as the Body of Christ, made up of the multitude of individual Christians. This viewpoint along with radical questioning about the heart and essence of Christianity very soon led to a reappraisal of Christology: it was no longer the glorified Christ, but the Jesus of history, his life, suffering and dying, the mystery of Jesus' life, that moved into the center of faith's awareness. Following in the train of this new ecclesial and Christological way of thinking came a fresh understanding of the form and content of the liturgy, especially in respect of the meaning and substance of the sacraments.

II

This all-embracing reform movement, with its growing inner dynamism leading to a fundamental renewal in the common awareness of faith, and at last receiving official ratification in the Second Vatican Council and the comprehensive reforms initiated by that council, provides the framework and background for the work of Odo Casel. He knew that his first duty was to his own time wherein he detected most notably a trend towards mystery. His real standpoint, which gave him and others their dominant orientation, was gained, however, by his deeper understanding of liturgical-sacramental action. The decisive impulse came from personal, spiritual experience within the celebration of the liturgy, which Casel would have us grasp intuitively as the whole liturgical-sacramental action, seen as the symbolically communicated, and real participation in, the sacramentally present Christ-event. This intuitive and pneumatic *gnosis* (beholding in faith) of the reality of faith did, however, have a prehistory, so that various factors contributed to this fresh statement of the theology of the mysteries.

In his formative years at the beginning of the twentieth century, Casel encountered a mainly cerebral and rationalistic theology, the so-called neo-scholasticism. In this, any feeling for the liturgy and its celebration or for its aesthetic and symbolic forms was lacking, as was also any sensitivity to the mystical or to mystery which, according to biblical and patristic usage, connoted the reality and the realization of the divine redemptive fact in Christ through the Church. Moreover, in this theology the sacrament was understood simply as a means of grace, a materially and objectively effective instrument which occasioned the communication of grace from God to man but which, in the final analysis, remained an abstract, incomprehensible entity. Furthermore, the structure of the Christian faith appeared as a building constructed out of a miscellany of equally important doctrinal propositions—almost limitless in number, it would seem—with their derivative moral system, so that the inner unity and existential impact of the Christian faith, its true center and essentially personal structure, had become totally lost to view. In a time of crisis such a theology is quite incapable of giving simple, convincing and enlightening answers to those seeking for what is central to the Christian faith.

It happened, therefore, that in expounding his basic theological conviction, Casel did not receive much of an impulse from the theology and Church of his time; his efforts became directed, rather, to "reform from the source." For this reason he turned to the writings of the Fathers and so gained access to an understanding of theology and liturgy. In these writings—he was convinced—theology had nothing at all to do with scholarly theory, but with *gnosis*, with a Spirit-mediated insight into the mystery of God and his redemptive work. Such an insight was inaccessible to discursive reasoning. This mystery had reached its historical summit in Jesus Christ, and this historical actualization in Christ's redemptive act becomes present anew in each sacramental action of the Church. On this view, the culmination of the reality of faith resides in the liturgical-sacramental action of the Church; all theology is a resonance from, and introduction to, the sacraments and an exposition of their mystery-content.

It is not grammatically formulated truths of faith nor abstract, theoretically constructed formulae, but the concrete, practically arranged fulfillment of sacramental actions that leads to the heart of the faith—an idea which is encapsulated in the phrase: "God-in Christ-through the Church." To base, in this way, the definition of the heart of Christianity upon the realist symbolism of sacramental action—that is upon the actual mediation of Christ's redemptive work through the sacraments—makes it possible for the individual Christian to participate in Christ's action, to become existentially conformed to Christ, to become an imitator, a true disciple of Christ; and this discipleship rests upon the sacraments.

III

The normative influence upon Casel, as he developed his central thoughts on the theology of mystery, was that of the early Church Fathers. He was convinced that their writings did not embody a speculative theology, nor were they expressions of private opinion; they represented the normative theology and doctrine that was binding, because given through the early Church. This theology was later superseded as a result of the prestige of scholasticism and then neo-scholasticism. For Casel the presence of the mystery of Christ's redemptive work in liturgy and sacrament became the center of the Christian faith-reality from which, more than from any other aspect of Christian life, there can be derived in a time of cultural crisis new perspectives, reliable signposts and true standards. Finally, the establishment of this turning towards liturgy produced other impulses which gave a new direction to the diffuse trends of the times. There emerged a sense of the law of form, of classic shape, of given objectivity—these things put a deep stamp upon liturgical action; there was encouragement of a sense of community among those taking part in the liturgy, of a communion that reached out into the universal community of the Church which supported and embraced the individual in the celebration of the liturgy and of the sacraments, and which broke through the boundaries of isolated subjectivity. Most important of all, within the liturgical-sacramental action there began to shine out the real shape of the Christ-event, that mystery which men and women can apprehend and participate in only by faith and which cannot, without losing its quality of mystery, be expressed in theoretical concepts.

In the more precise explication of this liturgical mystery-reality Casel found support from the history of religion, evidence of which he had already found in Patristic texts. The material had come to light through his postgraduate work on mystical silence in the Greek philosophers—a work which gained him a doctorate in philology in 1919. His first degree in 1912 followed his work on the eucharistic doctrine of St Justin Martyr. The parallel he had found in the history of religion was this: even though the Christian sacraments find their origin directly in Christ's action, nonetheless they display an astonishing closeness and structural similarity to the so-called mystery religions, the ideal type of which sets the basic pattern of sacramental action. This, however, achieves its full purity and perfection only in the performance of the Christian sacramental mysteries. Seen in this light, Casel defined "mystery" as "a sacred, cultic action, in which a redemptive fact is made present through ritual." By performing this ritual the worshipping community participates in the redemptive act and thereby finds salvation.

For Casel himself and for many others at that time this guide from the history of religion was significant and helpful in their understanding of the distinctiveness of sacramental action. Casel certainly used it only as a help, as a kind of general, anthropological pointer; but it led, and still leads, to a variety of misunderstandings. Again and again Casel has been falsely and damagingly interpreted as though he believed—as do some Evangelical theologians, chiefly of the history of religion school—that the Christian sacraments are derived simply from models found in the history of religion. In the last analysis his purpose was to smooth every possible way into the heart of the Christian faith, into the living celebration of the mysteries, that is of the sacraments, for the sake of a generation that had once again become sensitive to religion in general. Seen in this way, much of the misunderstanding of Casel's concern revealed a lack of sympathy for the needs of his times. Casel had been deeply sensitive to that need and had taken it into account in the working out of his theology of mystery.

IV

With commendable prudence, that great promoter of the liturgical movement in Germany, Abbot Ildefons Herwegen (1874-1946), allowed Casel the time and leisure to work at an adequate presentation of his pioneering essays in a new understanding of theology, Church and liturgy. From the time of publication of its first volume in 1921 until his untimely death in 1948, Casel was chief editor of the *Jahrbuch für Liturgiewissenschaft* (known since 1950 as *Archiv für Liturgiewissenschaft*), regarded in the German-speaking world as the preeminent liturgical journal. In numerous essays and a wealth of literary reports and reviews, accompanied by copious documentation from Patristic writings, he worked out the ground plan of his theology of mystery and stoutly defended the insight he had gained against all manner of attacks. This presentation of his trail-blazing, new theological evaluation not only gained for Casel and his theology the publicity it needed, but led also to one of the most important theological debates of the first half of the twentieth century which, thanks to Casel's spirited defence of his views in face of a multitude of misunderstandings, did not run out of steam until after his death.

From 1922 onwards the external conditions for this stupendous output was provided by the convent of Benedictine nuns of Herstelle (Weser), where Casel acted as spiritual director with great conscientiousness and untiring spiritual energy, until his sudden death on Easter morning 1948. In this convent Casel found not only the quiet and seclusion which enabled him to go on writing, all the while deepening his insight and effectively defending his theology of mystery, but also plenty of opportunity of casting his exalted theology into a simpler and more generally understandable mould. This opportunity was given by the addresses, lectures and so-called conferences, for which the sisters assembled, chiefly on Sundays and feast days, when the appropriate liturgical texts and scripture pericopes were expounded in the style of a modern sermon.

On these occasions Casel repeatedly demonstrated his ability to communicate the wealth of his theological knowledge, the depth of his personal liturgical experience, and the fullness of the idea of mystery in an arresting manner in simple words. Thanks to the circumstances of his life, we possess numerous brilliantly formulated texts of Casel's, unburdened of heavy quotations from the Fathers and free from any specialist discussion or polemical argument, but presenting concisely and vividly the central content of his theology of mystery.

V

The volume we have here provides a representative cross-section of the kind of texts mentioned above, arranged thematically, to show the mystery of Christ being made present and unfolding in the Christian Year. Casel related the concept of mystery to much more than the strict framework of sacramental action, allowing it to embrace the whole liturgy and especially the mystery of festivals. In doing this he was once again following the early Church's comprehensive understanding of mystery, and at the same time building a bridge across to the similar broad concept of mystery that is found in the eastern Church. Thus he understood the Christian Year as a single, whole mystery, as the making present of the one and for ever complete Christ-event, Sunday by Sunday, and on every feast day, although with varying accent from occasion to occasion. Casel's exposition of the several seasons and festivals of the Christian Year derives its impact and special claim not least from his emphatic assertion that within the Christian Year we find in the end "nothing new, but always the same thing." The texts in this volume give repeated evidence that the indivisible wholeness of the Christ-event, of the all-embracing quality of the mystery of Christ by no means gives a monotonous and slack character to his exposition of the Christian Year, but facilitates, rather, by the reciprocal interlocking of different feasts (e.g. Christmas in the light of the Cross; Easter under the sign of the Epiphany, etc.), a new and improved understanding of the Christian Year.

These essays display also the astonishing freshness and unfailingly creative power of Casel's work, the importance of which has been for the most part undervalued and scarcely ever mentioned. There can be no doubt that Casel's fundamental ideas and normative insights remained active and formative from the start, and in spite of much one-sided interpretation, remain so today. Whoever is able to read the signs of the times correctly will discover in the intellectual, political and ecclesial life of today many parallels with the years of that critical renascence, to which can be traced back the beginnings of Casel's theological thinking. Courage to face up to the problems of the times and to provide pointers in the right direction is demanded of the Church and of theology at the end of the twentieth century just as much as it was at the beginning of that century.

In looking back to the origins of ecclesial and theological renascence in Odo Casel, we must not complacently allow ourselves to rest in the enjoyment of those things in the life of faith which are now taken for granted, although their acquisition did not come about without much struggle and argument. We ought to see in this steadfast mentor and reformer that prophetic impetus which is valid far beyond his own time, and which points for us today the way to interpreting the signs of our times.

1
Making Present the Mystery of Christ

The meaning of the Christian Year

ONCE AGAIN our holy Mother Church begins a new year—the so-called Christian Year. Alongside the Christian Year we have the secular year; but we must take care that we do not casually place these two years in parallel, for they derive from two different worlds. Outwardly, it is true, they appear alike; both embrace a time-span of 365 days, that is 365 solar circuits or, in astronomical terms, 365 circuits of the earth around the sun. Already we can detect a difference. The secular year begins with the fresh ascent of the sun. December 25 is the *natalis solis invicti* the birthday of the invincible sun-god. Just before this the sun had reached its lowest point; but now it begins again to ascend in triumph: "the light increases."(1) In early antiquity people preferred to think that the year began in Spring. The Jews celebrated the Spring month of Nisan as the first month of the year; the Greeks had their *anthesterion*; the Romans celebrated 1 March as the beginning of a new year. The year was linked with the sun, and so with natural cosmic life. The secular year is cosmic; its repetition indicates the power of nature constantly to revive.

In the Christian Year too we find a link with the course of nature. Although the year has already begun on 1 December, that is only a preparation for the *natalis Domini*, for the birth of the Son of God and for his epiphany. 25 December and 6 January are also ancient sun festivals; but the Church does not interpret them cosmically or astronomically but pneumatically as symbols of a higher, divine world, of the cosmos of God, who is exalted above all times and is enthroned within an unchanging aeon. For this reason the Christian Year does not have to be too rigidly bound to astronomical dates, but may begin with the time of preparation—that is with Advent. The Epiphany of our Lord, however, is the true beginning of the year. Nonetheless the Christian Year still has a sense of a beginning in the spring. The Pasch is older than the Epiphany, and occurs in the spring, in the "first" month of the year, the time, early in the year, of the equinox. In the early Christian view, the world was created in all the adornment of springtime. Many dated the Creation on 25 March, and the same day was taken to be the day of redemption through the incarnation, the passion and resurrection of our Lord. On this day, either at the first full moon of spring or shortly after, the work of creation began, as did the work of re-creation. This day was the beginning of the secular year, of the year of redemption and also of the year of the mysteries. To this day a period of time was prefixed: two days, six days, forty days, but all of that was merely preparation. Everything was integrated into the holy Easter Vigil, with which the new aeon, the time of eternal life inaugurated by Christ, began. In this it is already evident that the natural year with its symbols from natural life had become the symbol of a higher, divine year. Christ is the New Year. His work of redemption is the content of the year of the mysteries. The year of the mysteries has to do not with temporal development, but with divine acts and divine things. But God is *eternity*, and so the Christian Year is the symbol of things that are not temporal but eternal. How can something temporal be a symbol of the eternal? Nature itself possesses a kind of eternity, because it is for ever recurring in the same forms. Therein, however, lies its bondage. The natural man is never able to escape from this eternally rolling treadmill. Even when he dies, his *natural* being is recycled, to become reborn again into the same treadmill. At all events, the ancients spoke of the wheel of fate, to which mankind is bound, just as the criminal is shackled to the wheel until his bones are broken. Escape from this oppression can be provided only by one who dwells outside the wheel in changeless, divine exaltation at the center of all being—that is by God alone. He leads us out from time into eternity: "He freed me, set me at large, he rescued me, since he loves me" (Ps 18:19).

Even more frightening than the ancient concept of the cyclical recurrence of time is the modern notion—that has held the field since the late Middle Ages—of time as a continuous forward movement, allowing of no turning back, no transformation, no recurrence. This concept has come to dominate modern, civilized man's philosophy of time and of the year. For industrial man, time is a line that stretches on endlessly and that is divided up into sections only by New Year celebrations. Each of these sections of time is hailed by the world as though it brought totally new things with it. This concept harmonizes comfortably with the idea of progress. The line proceeds not just forward but upward also. In the ascent, the old is discarded and there is always something new taking its place, until finally superman appears, endowed with the whole apparatus of technology. The most recent past has clearly demonstrated, however, that we are not witnessing an eternal, upward progress, but rather a slide downwards. Strange to say, since Nietzsche, alongside the modern view of time as a line, the notion of time as a never-ending recurrence of the same thing has gradually been gaining ground. What a comfortless thought, that all mankind's crimes and follies have to be repeated for ever and ever! However, it is true also that there are signs that the modern "scientific" concept of time no longer enjoys undisputed dominance.

The ancients had a fundamentally different concept of time. Ancient wisdom represented time as a snake which devoured its own tail—that is, returned into itself. For each individual, therefore, time is not a straight line but a circle or a cycle. But how can time return into itself? I can retrace my steps along the same road in space, but I cannot retrace my steps in time. Can God perhaps do that? "How can a grown man be born? Can he go back into his mother's womb and be born again?" (Jn 3:4). Jesus replied: "Do not be surprised when I say: You must be born from above. The wind blows wherever it pleases; you hear its sound, but you cannot tell where it comes from or where it is going. That is how it is with all who are born of the Spirit" (Jn 3:7f.). And then Nicodemus asked: "How can that be possible?" Jesus replied:

> You, a teacher in Israel and you do not know these things! I tell you most solemnly, we speak only about what we know and witness only to what we have seen and yet you reject our evidence. If you do not believe me when I speak about things in this world, how are you going to believe me when I speak about heavenly things? No one has gone up to heaven except the one who came down from heaven, the Son of Man who is in heaven (Jn 3:11).

For God, therefore, many things are possible that appear to be humanly impossible. Our example shows, however, that it is not a question of something *material* returning *in exactly the same form*. It is of no value to be born again of the flesh. But for what was born through the flesh to be reborn of the Spirit is an act of God. In this case something is being repeated, but on a higher plane. Development follows a circle, but unlike the snake it does not eat its own tail; it moves in a line that spirals higher and higher, winding itself up like a screw. It is not absolutely the same thing that recurs, nor is it something totally new that emerges: it is the eternal, divine idea that becomes realized in cyclical coils which rise up towards an immovable center, bearing within themselves some touch of the divine, as a symbol or as the way towards that changelessness into which they flow, like the screw, the point of which remains above, always in the same place, while the thread spirals upwards, ever and again returning on itself, each circle rising higher than the rest.

These reflections may help us understand the Christian Year better. This sacred Year emanates from a concept of time that differs from our human concept. The Christian Year is not a line but a circle. This Christian Year contains nothing new but always the same thing. We already know its full content. It has neither beginning nor end, but knows two points of departure: Epiphany and the Pasch; and these are also its summits. The mystery of Christ is always the same and always complete. It does not reveal itself bit by bit, but in its fullness. Development is human, fullness is divine. Today, on the first day of the Christian Year, we celebrate the entire mystery of redemption in the Eucharist. We may not say that the Epiphany cycle is the precondition of the Easter cycle. Both embrace essentially the same thing—seen from two different angles. The Christian could just as well begin with the Pasch and end with the Epiphany, which would then appear, more than it does at present, as Parousia. From this we can see already that the celebration of the Christian Year does not place circles *alongside* circles, but that cycles pile up upon each other, rising up in spirals, moving upwards as does a screw. We celebrate that which is the same and yet not the same. Always it is the old thing and yet always something new, the new thing. For it is the eternal, the divine, and the divine is ever young and new, because it is eternal *life*. An earthbound event dies in the moment that it occurs. The earthbound is superannuated. The ancients described the world as "ageing," as senile. Even the history of salvation under the old covenant fell prey to this ageing—it became the old covenant. "Now anything old only gets more antiquated until in the end it disappears" (Heb 8:13). God does not become old, because he is the fullness of life. He is *life itself.*

And when the life of God became revealed to us in Christ, the eternally coming One, the eternally new came down into our temporal sphere. With his resurrection a new aeon began, the aeon of eternity. It is true that in this aeon the Church and the Christian still have to make the effort to carry the cross, to be ready to suffer; but the Spirit is already present in the risen Christ and so within the aeon of God. Therefore, alongside the civic year the Year of the Lord, the year of aeonic life, takes its place. It is a symbol and sacrament of eternal life, moving in a circle. It is a symbol of the road to eternity and therefore moves like a screw upwards towards God. It moves—a symbol that eternal rest in God is not a state of numbed immortality, but an eternal triune life. It was Goethe who said:

> All effort, all struggle
> is eternal rest in the Lord God.

In a most wonderful way the Christian Year binds together the most energetic life of struggling and battling with divine contemplation and self-abnegation, thereby doing justice to our human nature. As Christians we are obliged to work, to struggle, to carry the cross, but always with the hope of victory. St Agnes said: "That which I desire, I already behold; that which I hope for, I already hold in my hand." Jesus Christ our Head is already throned at the right hand of the Father; in him we have already conquered, are already at rest with him. Nonetheless, the earthly part of us has still to prove itself in this present age.

For this reason the Christian Year displays to us the life, the struggles, the conquering of death, of our *Kyrios*, of our glorified Lord. He is not only our model, but fights *within us* and is *victorious in us*. His mystery is our way to the Father. The Christian Year is thus our real redemptive way of cyclic revolution round the sun that is Christ, a screw that raises us progressively higher above this earth, leading us to the unmoved peak—God the Father.

Alas for him who will not allow himself to be raised up, for him who thinks that nothing ever changes, so that he may quietly sink into apathy! No! Each fresh beginning of the Christian Year ought to find us at a higher level on the thread of the screw; otherwise we will remain in the world below, moldering away and ageing in our worldliness. "Lift up your hearts" our Lord commands; and in the collect of the last Sunday of the Christian Year we pray: "Lord, increase our eagerness to do your will and help us to know the saving power of your love." The *opus divinum*, the divine work of salvation, brings us grace but not for us do what we please with it; along with grace we are given a task. There is no turning back but only the striving to reach eternity. "Our salvation is even nearer than it was when we were converted" (Rm 13:11). Redemption's consummation is coming closer to us; let us go towards it not drowsily and lackadaisically, but awake and ready. An everlasting crown of victory awaits us if we have deliberately and fervently carried the crown of the Christian Year.

2
Advent

The life-style of a Christian

IDEAS WHICH PROVE to be genuinely fruitful and lasting usually turn out to be old ideas, indeed, ancient ideas. They are mankind's "primeval words" or, better perhaps, the words that God reveals to mankind. These words never lose their power, although they may temporarily become overlaid with apparently new ideas, which in the end turn out to be old ideas. Over and over again the ancient rocks rise above the torrents of time and demonstrate their impassive greatness. For a long time Advent had become no more than an atmospheric preparation for Christmas, which in turn had become seriously secularized. It was full of sentimentality and pious longing but lacked any clear concept or stimulus to the will. Today it means much more. This is the result of various new or, rather, old perceptions which once again have begun to illumine our minds. Every living truth has its day; suddenly new ideas, which for long have slumbered in twilight, are brought to light and reveal their healing power for the needs of the times.

Several factors have contributed to our fuller concept of Advent. First—and superficially it would seem—was research into the meaning of the word "advent." The history of religion, allied with philology, and especially the study of the cult of the ruler, have enabled us to appreciate once again the splendor that surrounds the word "advent." "Advent" is the Latin for the Greek "epiphany," "parousia," "epidemie"—words which all mean the luminous appearance of a god in the visible present, or at least the recognizable manifestation of his power; then it becomes applied to the approach of the divinely venerated king, emperor, and redeemer. The word also connotes the presence of divinity and, indeed, of a presence that manifests itself as succoring, saving, healing, liberating, cheering and illuminating. Therefore salvation is linked with advent. God emerges from his concealment and reveals his light, his power, and his supportive kindness to short-lived mortals. The word "advent" thus already connotes a certain materialization, a certain humanizing of the divine, which descends into the earthly sphere, but only in order to raise it up to itself. Epiphany is closely bound up with "mystery." Mystery, too, is a concept or fact, the deeper and more joyful content of which is being disclosed afresh in our own time. For too long people saw in mystery—if they did not disregard it altogether—nothing more than theological truth that was inaccessible to unaided reason; and that truth was regarded as but the residue of the ancient fullness of the Word. We have now come to appreciate once again that mystery is much more than that, that God's life itself is the mystery revealed in Christ: "No one has ever seen God; it is the only Son, who is nearest the Father's heart, who has made him known" (Jn 1:18). In particular, it is the redemptive action of God that is mystery, for it is in the redemptive act of Christ that the eternal *agape* of God has come down among us. "Behold the mystery of *agape*" then you will behold the heart of the Father, revealed to us by the only Son and none other. God himself is *agape* and it is out of his *agape* that he permits us to behold him. In his ineffable being he is Father; but in his compassion for us he became mother. Through *agape* the Father became feminine, the great sign of which is, that he begot from himself, and the fruit begotten from *agape* is *agape*. And for this reason too he came down to earth, assumed humanity and freely accepted the fate of mankind, so that he could identify with the weakness from which we, whom he loves, all suffer. And when he was about to offer himself in sacrifice and give himself as our ransom, he bequeathed to us a new covenant: My *agape* I give to you."(1) The Church is a mystery in that it is the "embodiment" of the action of Christ; for in her the grace of God shines out for the eyes of the world to see, now that Christ himself has ascended to the Father and is no longer visible to the world. In the cult-mysteries, however, he has left a pledge of his constant presence with the Church; in these mysteries it is he himself who is actively and salvifically present. Mystery is thus a continuous epiphany, a permanent advent of God in the world.

Connected to this is another perception which has become increasingly clear in our day. That is, that the kingdom of God is not exclusively something to be awaited in the future but is already with us; it is not just an object of faith and hope but a present reality. The writers of the holy scriptures of the new covenant, Paul and John in particular, and also the Fathers of the Church, notably the Alexandrian school, were convinced that in Christ we have already been given salvation, that the earnest given by the Holy Spirit guarantees to us the full wealth of glory. We are already in Christ and therefore in God; already, as Paul said with full assurance, we are seated at the right hand of God the Father in heaven: "But God loved us with so much love that he was generous with his mercy; when we were dead through our sins, he brought us to life through Christ—it is through grace that you have been saved—and raised us up with him and gave us a place with him in heaven, in Christ Jesus" (Eph 2:4-6). Our Lord's kingdom began at his resurrection; now he grants us a share in his risen life through the mysteries: "I tell you solemnly, if you do not eat the flesh of the Son of Man and drink his blood, you will not have life in you. Anyone who does eat my flesh and drink my blood has eternal life, and I shall raise him up at the last day" (Jn 53f.). This saying of our Lord tells us two things: we already enjoy divine life, but it is still to be revealed in its fullness, "living as we do by faith and not by sight" (2 Cor 5:7). With sighs we await the perfection of the kingdom of Christ; we still stand in crisis, awaiting the Judgment. The Christian's life is twofold: outwardly it stands under the Cross, inwardly it is a life of glory. And both of these are included in the concept of advent. Advent longs for the coming, and yet, through the assurance of faith and hope, already possesses that for which it longs; for Christ has appeared, while at the same time his glorious coming forms the substance of the Church's longing. Describing the perfect Christian, Clement of Alexandria wrote:

> He rejoices in his present inheritance, while at the same time is filled with delight at the prospect of the good things that are promised, for these are already with him. They are not hidden from him as though still absent, for he has already experienced what they are like. He is convinced through *gnosis* of what each of the expected gifts is like, and so he already possesses them.(2)

One catches sight of the emperor from afar; he is there and he is coming. We cry out to Christ: "Blessed is he who comes!" and in the mysteries we greet him as the One who has come.

These thoughts bring us into contact with eschatology as understood in the New Testament, that is with the doctrine of the Last Things, which for early Christians embraced not only death, judgment, heaven and hell, but proclaimed primarily the glorious coming of the rule of God upon earth, a coming which had begun at Christ's coming in the flesh and will be perfected in his coming in glory. In breathless suspense and with fervent longing, the early Christians awaited the full revelation of Christ's royal glory in the *parousia*. This would be the triumph of God and hence of righteousness, of truth and of love; it would spell the annihilation of the world that fought against God, and it would usher in the exaltation of the *ecclesia* of the elect. The Middle Ages drifted further and further away from this New Testament eschatology as a result, no doubt, of a certain earthly realization of the kingdom of God in the rule of the Pope and the Holy Roman Emperor. This caused hope for the eschatological kingdom to recede. The triumphalist individualism of the post-Gothic and Renaissance period finally and thoroughly extinguished the Church's expectation of universal salvation through the *parousia*. From that time onwards the Christian's effort was directed towards salvation of the individual soul through the cultivation of personal union with God. Our generation once again is aware of community, of nation, of mankind, but has secularized the eschatological hope and, in spite of all disillusion, strives to build a kingdom of blessedness on this earth. Christendom now, in contrast, must turn again towards the eschatological concept of the kingdom of Christ, which expects nothing from this world but all from God. As has been said, the New Testament is full of this joyous hope in the consummation of God's rule in the *parousia* of the Lord who will then complete the work begun in his first *parousia*. "The Lord is very near" (Phil 4:5)—this is the cry on the lips of the Church as she advances to meet her Lord. Christ will usher in the kingdom of righteousness and everlasting peace. It is not, however, as though the kingdom subsisted in hope alone; the kingdom of God already within us, not a kingdom of this world, of outward displaying of might, but a kingdom of the Spirit. The Lord already comes to us in the Spirit, in mystery. "We are already the children of God but what we are to be in the future has not yet been revealed" (Jn 3:2). Expectation and fulfillment marry; hope and possession, *pistis* and *agape* unite—and that, as we have already discovered, is the characteristic of Advent.

These preliminary observations are sufficient to show that Advent is a lot more than a preparation for Christmas; that the reality behind the word embraces all that is meant by the broadest Christian interpretation of Epiphany, and this is expressed liturgically in Advent in the narrower sense, in the feast of the Nativity, and in the feast of the Epiphany. Indeed, originally it included the Church's expectation of the *parousia*, which note is still clearly sounded in the feast of the Epiphany and also in Advent. "Advent" is thus the correct name for the whole of the first season of the Christian Year up to the preparation for the Pasch. In fact in a certain sense it applies to the whole Christian Year, because the Pasch itself is an expectation of the *parousia*, and not just an expectation, but also its first pneumatic realization; for by his resurrection and ascension the Lord has entered into that eternal glory into which one day he will lead home his whole Church. "Jesus who has been taken up from you into heaven, this same Jesus will come back in the same way as you have seen him go there" (Acts 1:11). The early Church celebrated the Easter Vigil as a waiting for the coming of the Lord; the Church today concludes the Christian Year with the day of the Lord's *parousia* as it also begins Advent with the Gospel of the Second Coming.

In this way the entire Christian Year is contained within the framework of Advent. Advent in the narrower sense, however, embraces the whole, by way of preparation; it leads us towards the Epiphany, that is to the appearance of the Lord in this world. Epiphany has two phases: first, the coming of the Lord in the flesh of sinful man, in weakness and insignificance, that begins with his birth and ends on the Cross—"from birth to sign" as Clement of Alexandria put it;(3) second, the coming in glory, the glory of the Cross, manifested in his resurrection and ascension, known to us through faith, and to be revealed to all the world at his Second Coming—the *parousia*. His first coming was not an epiphany in the full sense, for the Lord's glory was still hidden; he appeared in sinful flesh. "God dealt with sin by sending his Son in a body as physical as any sinful body" (Rm 8:3). This was God's decree. "As it was his purpose to bring a great many of his sons into glory, it was appropriate that God, for whom everything exists and through whom everything exists, should make perfect, through suffering, the leader who would take them to their salvation" (Heb 2:10). Only after the Lord had atoned for sin through the Cross could the glory of divinity totally suffuse his humanity and make him a living Spirit. "Now this Lord is the Spirit" (2 Cor 3:17). From time to time even before the Resurrection, glimpses of his glory shone out, as at the Transfiguration and in his miracles. On these occasions the man Jesus was revealing himself as the Son of God, as Christ the Lord. The baptism of Jesus in particular was an epiphany or theophany, that is, an appearance of God to the eyes of the world. In a voice from heaven the Father acknowledged Jesus as his Son, and the Spirit descended upon him in bodily form. That is why John the Baptist pointed Jesus out as the long-awaited One, as the Son of God and the Lamb of God, who takes away the sin of the world. This is precisely what constitutes the liturgical Advent. In the Gospel passages for Advent, John the Baptist leads us up to a point immediately before our Lord's public appearance. The line along which Advent moves cannot but end in the baptism of Christ, seen as the beginning of his redemptive life. The baptism, however, is only a beginning, pointing ahead to an even greater baptism, for which the Lord himself is longing, and which will be accomplished on the Cross in his blood. For this reason John describes the One he is baptizing as "the Lamb of God" (Jn 1:29 & 36). The baptism in the Jordan thus becomes a prefiguring of the baptism on the Cross; the Epiphany finds its perfect consummation in the Pasch. In this way the feast of the Epiphany is able to celebrate the whole of redemption, because the baptism in the Jordan points forward to the Cross.

There is a second line, however, running through Advent. This line runs through to Christmas as the birthday of Christ, and it is disclosed mainly in the Gospels telling of the virgin motherhood of Mary. This line is evident also in several of the texts in the Divine Office. The line has to end in the birth of the Infant Jesus; but this culminating point is no mere idyll, as might often appear, to judge by the poetry associated with Christmas; it is, rather, a pointer towards the Cross, for the Lord is portrayed as a weak, poor child, unrecognized and persecuted by the world. He assumed a lowly body that he might offer it up on the Cross. "This is what he said on coming into the world: 'You who wanted no sacrifice or oblation, prepared a body for me. You took no pleasure in holocausts or sacrifices for sin'; then I said, '...God, here I am! I am coming to do your will' " (Heb 10:5-7). In this way the birth of our Lord is incorporated into the mystery of redemption.

Rome, it is true, seems for some time to have celebrated 25 December, the precise date, indeed, and without an associated octave, as simply the day of our Lord's birth—even though this date was not originally chosen as our Lord's historical birthday. The Roman Church, however, soon came to recognize, that this was no true mystery, and so it developed the festival of Christmas as a fully-blown mystery to celebrate the coming of the royal Son of God. This is clearly demonstrated by the three Christmas Masses and by all of the Divine Office for Christmas. As a result, even to the present day, the Roman feast of the Epiphany bears a secondary character, whereas in the East, where originally it was the only feast of the Incarnation, it incorporates the whole splendor of the mystery. Today one can perceive in the Roman liturgy, that the Epiphany is more than just the adoration of the Magi, for the Epiphany liturgy associates the adoration of the Magi with the baptism in the Jordan and the miracle at Cana, when for the first time Jesus let his glory be seen (antiphon for the *Benedictus* and for the second antiphon for the *Magnificat*). The two feasts, Christmas and Epiphany, complement each other; but both point beyond to the great feast of the Pasch, which they partially anticipate.

Advent in the broad sense is a whole mystery, for in its liturgy it sets out sacramentally the redemptive work of Christ, enabling us to enter into it with a living participation, and so find salvation. In this first division of the Christian Year we contemplate the redemptive action of our Lord above all from the point of view of the Incarnation of the *logos*, the appearance of God in the flesh, while at the same time we do not exclude the redeeming death of Christ but, rather, celebrate the final fruit of that death in the glorious return of our Lord. We anticipate this event, which has not yet been historically enacted—just as we celebrate the Lord's Incarnation which has already happened—in terms of its full effect and not just in its beginnings. Clearly demonstrated here is the fact, that the mystery always embraces the completed work of redemption, the *oikonomia*, because otherwise it would not guarantee total redemption.

How can the mystery give us that which has not yet arrived at historical fulfillment? Herein lies the amazing power of the mystery. The mystery is the totality of the divine reality, still concealed under symbols, not yet manifest but containing all of God's grace. As the pledge of the Spirit—of which Paul often speaks—it gives us certainty of the glory that is to come, and so assures us of total salvation.

In the narrower sense too Advent is also mystery, for we cannot transpose ourselves back into the period before the Redemption. Therefore Advent's cries of longing are not to be taken literally. We have been redeemed, we are members of Christ and of his Church, daily celebrating his redemptive act at the altar. If during Advent we look towards Christ and long for his coming, we do so on the strength of his first coming. Full of confidence we cry out, "Come!" because he has already come. We want his coming to blossom into a complete Epiphany, to become fully realized in us; we want the Church to perfect herself in all her members until the "Day of Christ." Although his glorious coming has not yet been accomplished historically, on Christmas Eve we sing: "He is here" (Ps 96:1) because his second advent is unequivocally guaranteed by his first. Through this twofold thought—that he is to come and that he has come—Advent becomes a characterization of the Christian life.

The Christian lives in two worlds. In terms of his body and historical existence he inhabits this aeon, this temporal sphere that still stands under the sign of sin and still sighs for salvation. But according to the Spirit, that is his supernatural existence, he is already living in the kingdom of Christ, in the aeon that is to come, under the sign of God's rule. He is "in Christ" and Christ is in him. The mystery of the new Covenant is indeed expressed in Paul's words: "Christ in you," but Paul immediately adds: "your hope of glory" (Col 1:27). Our glory is still hidden, is still only a germ or a foundation, but it is a foundation which, like an ear of corn, contains the whole plant. In this way the Christian life corresponds to the twofold Advent of Christ, as Paul describes it in his letter to the Philippians:

> In your minds you must be the same as Christ Jesus:
> His state was divine
> yet he did not cling
> to his equality with God
> but emptied himself
> to assume the condition of a slave,
> and became as men are;
> and being as all men are,
> he was humbler yet,
> even to accepting death,
> death on a cross.
> But God raised him on high
> and gave him the name
> which is above all other names
> so that all beings
> in the heavens, on the earth and in the underworlds,
> should bend the knee at the name of Jesus
> and that every tongue should acclaim
> Jesus Christ as Lord,
> to the glory of God the Father (Phil 2:5ff.).

The Lord's two appearances are closely bound up with each other: their point of intersection is the Cross. Only through the Cross could Christ be exalted. If we want to share in the Lord's glorious *parousia*, we must humble ourselves here and now alongside the Infant of Bethlehem, must share in his abandonment and poverty, and must carry the Cross. Only then can we be sure that as Jesus, who appeared to the world as the poor

Infant of Bethlehem and died on the Cross will appear as the Christ of glory, the *kyrios*, so will we appear openly with him in glory (Col 3:4).

It has now become clear what the liturgy of Advent really is. It unites the two sides of the mystery. The Gospel of the First Sunday in Advent presents the overwhelming picture of the return of our Lord to judge the world and to redeem his faithful: "Stand erect, hold your heads high, because your liberation is near at hand" (Lk 21:28). The Advent hymn, too, *Conditor alme siderum*, tells both of the birth of the Lord in this world's evening, and the glorious advent of the Judge, before whose mighty power every knee will bend. On the second and third Sundays of Advent the Baptist steps onto the scene, not to point to the Child in the Crib, but to the Lamb of God who takes away the sin of the world and also to execute judgment on the earth. "He will baptize you with the Holy Spirit and fire. His winnowing fan is in his hand; he will clear his threshing floor and gather his wheat into the barn; but the chaff he will burn in a fire that will never go out" (Mt 3:11f.). This is how John saw both aspects of Christ's coming at one glance.

The Cross of Christ hangs invisibly over Advent, and to the early Christians Christmas was the "sign of his coming" (cf. Mt 24:3), the "sign of the Son of Man" (Mt 24:30). For the faithful it will be a sign of triumph, for the wicked a sign of damnation. In this life, however, the Cross must be the sign of repentance, hence the penitential character of Advent in the West. Through the Cross our wills must be purified and brought into line with the will of God. In the Lord's Prayer we pray daily for the advent of the kingdom: "Thy kingdom come" and we add: "thy will be done on earth as it is in heaven." This prayer will finally be answered on the Day of Christ, when God will establish his dominion over all things. In the meantime we have to strive to realize God's will in ourselves and in this world. If with sacrifice we have fought for this, then the advent of God will be our victory too. The things which on earth seemed very hard to bear, because we were not privy to the decrees of God, will be revealed to us when he comes, as the way he was leading us in love. If on earth we stand under the cross of the will of God, our life becomes a continuous ascent until the manifesting of the kingdom of God. Just as the Sundays in Advent draw nearer to the Christmas mystery, while at the same time they ascend towards Epiphany, so our life is no passing away into earthly, natural growing, maturing and decaying, but an ascent towards the Bridegroom, who is approaching in all his splendor. "The Lord is very near" (Phil 4:5). His radiance is already shining out upon us, filling us with new hope and a new life beyond all our imagining, lifting us up from the earth's trough and permitting us to share in the life of God now.

All of this is given us not as individuals but within the fellowship of the Church, which as his Bride is on pilgrimage towards the Lord. This was the way the early Church walked, in holy fellowship, towards her *kyrios*, already aware, through the Spirit, that she shone in the light of Advent. The Church does not walk alone; the Lord is with her, he is in her. The individual Christian, however, feels safe within the Church. Even if in this aeon man has to travel alone along the road to death he is not severed from the holy community, and the hope of all is directed to the communal resurrection at the *parousia* of the Lord. Death and decay are part of the penitential character of Advent in this life; but this must not cause us to close our eyes to the glory that is promised us, already stored up for us in the kingdom. In this way, if with the Spirit of the Lord in our hearts, and in communion with the Church, we celebrate Advent, it will be for us a sure pledge that at length, on the Day of his glorious coming, the full glory of our *kyrios* will shine out upon us.

3
Christmas

The Mystery of the Incarnation

CHRISTMAS IS NOT the celebration of the nobility of human nature, nor is it an indulgence in childhood memories and tender human affection, nor is it even a festival of the Child Jesus, smiling at us from the lap of his sweet mother, telling us of the love of God. It is much more than all of that; it is the living and overwhelming presence of God among men. The eternal majesty of the eternal Godhead before whom every creature in its nothingness breathes in awe, that divine majesty whom no human eye has ever seen or can see, who is separated from mankind by an infinite eternity, and yet to whom the creature is drawn by every thread of spiritual desire—that majesty has come among us, has permitted us to gaze upon his countenance and to recognize in the face of the Lord and King the features of the Father.

At Christmas there comes to pass that for which mankind has longed since time began, something that lay beyond his reach and for which he could do no more than hope. All of human history is but a thirsting for a sight of the Father's face, a desire to rest in the ultimate source and end of our being. Moses entreated the Lord: "Let me look upon your glory" (Ex 33:18), but the Lord did not let him see his face, but only a shimmer of his back as he passed by. Even that much filled the beholder with boundless blessedness. The psalmist cried out: "Listen, O shepherd of Israel, who lead Joseph like your flock and are throned above the cherubim. Appear! Show your power and come to save us! Show us your face and we shall be saved" (Ps 79:1ff.).

The prophets promised that the Lord would make himself present; to the expectant congregation they proclaimed:

> Arise, shine out, for your light has come,
> the glory of Yahweh is rising on you,
> though night still covers the earth
> and darkness the people.
> Above you Yahweh now rises
> and above you his glory appears.
> No more will the sun give you daylight,
> nor moonlight shine on you,
> but Yahweh will be your everlasting light,
> your God will be your splendor (Is 60:1f. and 19).

It was not only those enlightened by God's preparatory revelation, but the pagans too, who called upon their gods to come among them; in so doing they were implicitly calling upon the true God for whom they thirsted, and whom they dimly discerned behind the wilderness of their idols. In this phenomenon, the dream of fulfillment of this longing took forms which the strict Semite, with his sharp distinction between God and the world, did not comprehend, and which could not become reality until the Incarnation of the Son of God. The hymns and secret rites of the mystery religions show a feeling for the Epiphany, that is for a visible, palpable, enlightening and salvific coming of God. "Come, O our hero Dionysius, to your holy temple!"(1) "Do you not see, O son of

Zeus, Dionysius, how your prophets are in distress? Come, O you of the golden countenance, come down from Olympus, swinging the thurible, Lord, ruler, come to us your devoted band." And when the god revealed himself in some mighty act of deliverance, the faithful sank, trembling, to the ground. "Cast yourselves to the ground, throw your trembling limbs onto the earth, for the ruler, the son of Zeus is entering his palace." Or one can hear the voice of the god resounding in the ether; a powerful light streams out and sets the heaven and earth aflame; all nature keeps silent, the leaves on the trees cease their murmuring and the animals are struck dumb before the presence of the divinity.(2) These were the wishful dreams of something that was to become reality in a totally different fashion.

When God had fulfilled the longing of the pagans and realized the promises made to his own prophets, everything was quite different from what men and women had imagined. God's thoughts are always quite different from mankind's concepts. To begin with they seem to fall short of these concepts, but in fact they surpass them by a heaven's-breadth. God came as man and revealed his love for mankind in the face of a man, of a child no less. He did not come in fearsome majesty, in a light that flooded the world, in obvious power and glory, but in weakness and helplessness, despised even and abandoned. He came secretly, not declaring omnipotence and vaunting wisdom, not as judge of the wicked and champion of the righteous, ushering in his victorious kingdom. No, he came in order to reveal *agape*, that is the self-giving love that is found in God alone. This is the summit of the Christian mystery of wisdom: God is *agape*, and this *agape* shines out for us in the face of a man, of the kindest, most unselfish, most amiable and most sacrificial of all men.

Is not the Christmas mystery, nonetheless, a revelation of the noblest in human nature, of the "philanthropy" of which St Paul writes in Titus 3:4? Is not Christmas man's celebration of his own humanity, which sees its noblest qualities personified in the Child in the Crib?

No. That would be totally to misunderstand Christmas; it would be to drag this sublime mystery down from heaven to earth and to idolize mankind. In our times, however, mankind's self-idolization has come drastically to grief. The "good" human being, so much cultivated and cosseted since the Renaissance and the Enlightenment, has bared all too clearly the fangs of the predatory beast. How are we to be redeemed from the curse of the world if Christmas is no more than a festival of humanity?

No. This child, this man, from whose face the kindness of God shines upon us is God. He is the Son, consubstantial with the Father. "The *logos* was made flesh, he lived among us and we saw his glory" (Jn 1:14). The God-man is the supreme revelation of God. "No one has ever seen God; it is the only Son, who is nearest the Father's heart, who has made him known" (Jn 1:18). It is only faith in the divinity of this man, born of a woman on Christmas night, that brings salvation and satisfies our desire to look upon the Father's face.

"To have seen me is to have seen the Father" (Jn 14:9). Christ the God-man is the primary symbol, the original and ultimate mystery. A symbol is genuine if we can see through the image and possess the reality behind it. A mystery is genuine if in the symbol and word we are able to grasp the ultimate mystery. So it is with our Lord Jesus Christ. "It is the same God that said, 'Let there be light shining out of darkness', who has shone in our minds to radiate the knowledge of God's glory, the glory on the face of Christ" (2 Cor 4:6).

This vision is, however, a vision in faith. The eye of flesh, even of the mind, sees only the weakness and helplessness of Christ and of his chosen flock, the Church. Neither his glory nor his Church's glory has yet been openly declared. We still walk through a world of sin. The world, which proudly turns away from God, cannot look upon the infinite purity of the face of God; were it to do so it would die, melt away like wax before a fire. For this reason God has hidden his face—out of mercy, but also in judgment. At his first coming he assumed sinful flesh, beneath which divinity was concealed, allowing only glowing sparks to spurt out from time to time. He did this so as to be able to give himself up in death for sin. We have to follow him in his voluntary humiliation. From us he demands the sacrifice of faith, that is we must surrender our own ego, destroy our pride and open ourselves up to the divine light that wants to fill us with grace. Sheer human nature with its self-assurance must die; but if we then press on obediently through the half-light of faith, the light of God is unveiled for us. We come to recognize in this man bowed down with grief, in this Child of Bethlehem, in the Crucified on Golgotha, the King of Glory, the Light of Divine Wisdom, the power of God that conquers the world.

When we celebrate Christmas we ought not to remain static before the Crib: we should contemplate the *whole* manifestation of God. If we do this the event of that holy night will become disclosed to us in its full supra-historical, eternal significance, as the appearing of God in this world, as the unveiling of his face—as *epiphany*. It is only the faithful soul, the mystic, who has an eye for this reality, for only he can see Christmas as it really is: the beginning and the foundation of God's supreme act which transforms the world and leads it towards its eternal consummation. Since that holy night God has been in the world and the world in God. *He is here*. The world now has a task before it. No longer is it going astray but is finding its way back to God, a way upon which the world will prove itself worthy of the great mysteries of dedication to God.

"Yahweh is in his holy Temple" (Ps 11:4). The temple of the Lord who has appeared in flesh is the community of those who have been embraced in his presence, the souls of the faithful, that is the Church. The Lord lives in her through his pneumatic presence, a presence that transcends all earthly modes of being; it is a divine presence, and so confers upon us a share in the very essence of God. In his Church God is *active*, healing, teaching, strengthening, enlightening and sanctifying. These effects he has, however, linked principally with the mysteries, which we celebrate in divine worship.

It was not the Lord's intention simply to come into human history and stay for a while among us then to leave us and continue his rule from on high. He said: "I am with you always; yes, until the end of time" (Mt 28:20). He is active among us through his *pneuma*, that is through his actual, divine power which pours out upon us from the glorified Christ. But he confirms his presence, making it available and palpable through external signs, recognizable by our senses, through sacred symbols—the sacraments in particular, which not only educate us to understand his salvific purposes, mediating his power as from a distance, but contain his immediate, living presence, placing us right at the heart of the salvation that flows from this presence. Just as he himself as God and man is the archetypal symbol, so that in the man Jesus we see the Father, in the same manner, in the symbols he has filled with his power and presence we possess *him* in all his redemptive power, which continues to be effective down the centuries through these symbols, for ever creating new life and perfecting that life.

In no way do we lag behind Jesus' contemporaries. Not at all—his Incarnation, his sacrifice, his exaltation are immediately present and available to us by faith and faith's vision, through the mysteries. If we celebrate the holy mysteries in true faith as mystics and co-workers—and such cooperation is the privilege of every one of the faithful in virtue of his living membership through baptism and confirmation in the pneumatic Body of Christ—we stand right at the heart of Christ's redemptive work. He takes hold of us and we are transformed by him. Through the ecclesial mystery we enter into the immediate and living presence of the archetypal mystery, that is of the revelation of God and his redemptive act. It no longer appears in historical events. Indeed from the start it never became exhausted in historical events, but was perfected in supra-historical reality.

The exaltation of the Lord, his entry into the heavenly sanctuary to ascend his throne at the right hand of the Father is no longer an historical happening but a supernatural reality. In the mystery, however, we perceive our Lord's total act of redemption, which began in the bright light of history to be completed in the inaccessible light of the eternity of God. We now see the birth of the Child in Bethlehem as the procession of the *logos*, the Son of God out from the eternity of the Father and from the eternal rest of the Trinity into our created world of time. The purpose of this was to lead our world back into its being in God. No longer do we regard Christ's dying on the Cross as the death of a condemned man, but as his mighty, total sacrifice for the redemption of mankind, and as his return, as perfect man and perfecter of his Church, to God the Father. His Resurrection, at the time known only to a few chosen persons, now becomes known to us through Faith's vision. With the eye of faith we see the exalted One at the right hand of the Father. Through faith we already possess that which has not yet been historically accomplished—his coming again in glory at the consummation of the world in the fullness of God's kingdom.

Through the mysteries we become immersed in the fullness of the reality of the Redeemer, in the power of his Incarnation, in the saving blood of his sacrifice, and in the transfiguring glory of his Resurrection. By this means we are drawn into Christ's innermost life; we share in his power, in his wisdom, in his *pneuma*; thus we become his Body which shares in his life and are thereby divinized and raised to the status of true people of God. We acquire the ability to survive in this temporal life with all its privation and misery, its persecution of the good and triumph of the wicked, with its pain and sickness and death; we can survive because by our superior existence we possess a new form of life—the life of Christ.

If we celebrate Christmas in this way along with mother Church, we celebrate the holy night truly, that is as the consecrated night, the night of the holy mother, when earth fades out of sight and unending divine life is born for us. Mary, the virgin mother is the symbol for us of holy virgin mother Church, who bestows on us true life. Jesus is for us the Child in whose image we are all born and in whom we all grow towards the full stature of Christ. In the holy mystery-Word, of which the Church says in this night—quoting from the prophet Isaiah—that it "endures for ever" (Is 10:9), and in the mystery-action of the sacrifice and sacrificial meal, we come into that blessed and sanctifying inheritance, designed and provided for us by God's grace as a Christmas gift, all of which is summed up in the words: "Behold, I am here."

4
Christmastide

The Crib and the Cross

IN THE GLOW OF MYSTERY that surrounds the night of our Lord's nativity, the Church proclaims: "The Word was made flesh, he lived among us, and we saw his glory, the glory that is his as the only Son of the Father, full of grace and truth" (Jn 1:14). At the Epiphany the Bride, who is the Church, takes up the cry of the prophet and encourages herself: "Arise, shine, Jerusalem... (Is 60:1f.). The evangelist and the prophet join in proclaiming that the glory of Christ is to be seen in the *ecclesia*; and the liturgy tells us that this all happens in the mystery of Christmas.

What does this mean? Does it mean that we already see the eternal light of God, that we perceive with eyes of faith—for the flesh is of no use here—the ineffable glory of the everlasting God? The same John tells us:

> My dear people, we are already the children of God but what we are to be in the future has not yet been revealed; all we know is that when he is revealed we shall be like him because we shall see him as he really is (1 Jn 3:2).

That is to say we do not yet look upon the undivided and unveiled glory of God. Even so, it was while still on earth that John had written "We saw his glory" (1 Jn 14). John said, too, that Isaiah's words concerning the unbelief of the Israel in his own time had been fulfilled in the unbelief of the Jews. In his vision, Isaiah declared: "Make the heart of this people gross, its ears dull; shut its eyes, so that it will not see with its eyes, hear with its ears, understand with its heart, and be converted and healed" (Is 6:10). John continues: "Isaiah said this when he saw his glory, and his words referred to Jesus" (Jn 12:41), that is to the Christ. According to John, Isaiah's vision was a vision of the Christ, not a vision of the eternal glory of God *per se*, but a prophetic vision of the Son of Man who was to come. It was not the "inaccessible light" of the Godhead that was seen, the light "whom no man has seen and no man is able to see" (1 Tim 6:16). Note well, no "man," that is no mere man, not, however, the divinized man who is no longer mere man; and what is seen is the glory of Christ, the glory of the incarnate Son of God. That is why John writes: The Word was made flesh...and we saw his glory." Revelation of divine glory is bound up with the Incarnation of the *logos*. The evangelist narrates:

> In the countryside close by there were shepherds who lived in the fields and took it in turns to watch their flocks during the night. The angel of the Lord appeared to them and the glory of the Lord shone round them.... The angel said... "Today a savior has been born to you; he is Christ the Lord. And here is a sign for you: you will find a baby wrapped in swaddling clothes and lying in a manger." And suddenly with the angel there was a great throng of the heavenly host, praising God and singing:
>
> Glory to God in the highest,
> and peace to men who enjoy his favour.
>
> So they hurried away and found Mary and Joseph, and the baby lying in a manger. When they saw the child they repeated what they had been told about him... (Lk 2:8-17).

Here we find a remarkable interweaving of sheer humanity and weakness with divine glory. Likewise in the account of the Magi: they come to do homage to a king, and they find a little child, a boy whom nonetheless they venerate as a God-king (cf. Mt 2:1-12). Is this "glory," which according to John and the prophets and the liturgy of Christmas and Epiphany we are supposed to see, of any real account? What sort of glory is that—a cave in a field, a manger, a little, crying baby and a poor couple, Mary and Joseph and some simple shepherds! This is all very human—and no doubt about it.

And yet John, the trustworthy evangelist tells us: "The Word was made flesh and we saw his glory."

We are compelled, therefore, to reorganize our thinking. When we use the word "glory" we think of splendor, pomp, majesty, blazing light, or we think of the limitless ecstasy of the divine light of eternity, which we depict according to human values and in earthly colors as something infinitely magnificent, powerful, mysterious and infused with the deepest wisdom and knowledge.

The glory of God is something quite different, infinitely deeper and finer, towering far above all power and wisdom. Paul taught us about it when he wrote to the Corinthians who were seeking the glory of wisdom and *gnosis*. He said:

> The language of the Cross may be illogical to those who are not on the way to salvation, but those of us who are on the way see it as God's power to save.... Do you see now how God has shown up the foolishness of human wisdom? If it was God's wisdom that human wisdom should not know God, it was because he wanted to save those who have faith through the foolishness of the message that we preach. And so, while the Jews demand miracles and the Greeks look for wisdom, here are we preaching a crucified Christ, a Christ who is the power and the wisdom of God. For God's foolishness is wiser than human wisdom, and God's weakness is stronger than human strength (1 Cor 1:18ff.).

Here we have the definitive words: it is the Crucified who is the Lord of Glory, the One whom we acclaim in the *Te Deum*—*Tu Rex gloriae, Christe*—"You are the King of Glory, O Christ!" In this we gain a totally new concept of glory. Glory is not the might of this world, nor is it the wisdom of this world. Glory derives from the Cross. The Cross gives the lie to all that speaks of this world and its glory; for the Cross judges and destroys all the might, the pride and the knowledge of this world. And yet, precisely through this contradiction the Cross empowers man to recognize and acquire the true glory that belongs to God. And so the Crucified is truly the King of Glory. From now on he possesses the glory of the Father: We acclaim "Jesus Christ as Lord, to the glory of God the Father" (Phil 2:11). Whoever confesses: "Jesus is Lord"—that is, that Jesus who humbled himself to become man and was nailed to the Cross is Lord—is a Christian, for he has recognized what genuine glory is. He has recognized that such glory has nothing in common with the earthly, human, self-centered, proud, vain and empty greatness of this world. By contrast it arises out of the death of this world, out of being crucified to this world. Whoever is able to say: "I hang with Christ on the Cross" (Gal 2:19) can see the glory of Christ. This, moreover, is the essence of faith. Faith is blind to external glory, to earthly knowledge, but has the ability to see through the apparent debasement of the Cross to its interior glory. Unbelief is able to see only the glory of the flesh, the aspirations of this world, for its eyes are eyes of flesh; but whoever has mortified the flesh attains faith: he sees the divine foundations of things, he sees past created things to their source in God, from whom created things derive their full meaning and beauty. Thus only through faith do external things begin to shine with true glory. The Cross, the humility of faith, is the one and only way towards the glory of God.

In this way we have solved the problem that was raised at the beginning of this chapter. In Christmas and at Epiphany we do behold the glory of God, the eternal light, for we see the glory through the humility of faith, and so see through and beyond the lowliness of the flesh. "The Word was made flesh." For the world, the becoming flesh of the Word was the only road leading to the vision of glory. "All flesh is grass and its beauty like the flower's...but the word of our God remains for ever" (Is 40:6, 8). But because this flesh, despite its transience, took pride in itself and exalted itself against God, God abased himself and appeared in "sinful flesh" (Rom 8:3). He bore our burdens and our weaknesses; he manifested the weakness of the flesh in himself. Out of evil he created good. Through sin, weakness took possession of all flesh, bringing sickness and death. And so in his *agape* God sent his Son "in a body as physical as any sinful body" (Rom 8:3), burdening him with the weight of sin and death. Now, whoever confesses that this poor, afflicted man of sorrows, the Cross-bearer, is Lord, already possesses the spiritual sight that is able to see the glory of the Cross (Rom 10:9; 1 Cor 12:3; Phil 2:11). This is the paradox of Christianity: glory out of insult, life out of death, light from darkness. True glory is *agape*; God's innermost being is *agape*; and all his might, wisdom, kingdom—all that makes up his glory—makes sense and has foundation only in *agape*. The ultimate reason, therefore, for his having revealed his glory through weakness is his own essence, that is, *agape*. This *agape* is his *doxa*, his glory. For this reason the King of Glory is called also the "Son of *agape*"(Col 1:3).

We do not gaze, therefore, upon the brightness of God, but see him through the medium of his appearance in the flesh. This flesh is initially like a veil, a curtain, but a curtain leading into the Holy of Holies: "In other words, brothers, through the blood of Jesus we have the right to enter the sanctuary, by a new way which he has opened for us, a living opening through the curtain, that is to say, his body" (Heb 10:19f.). The way in which this curtain discloses the Holy of Holies to us is described in John (1:18): "No one has ever seen God; it is the only Son, who is nearest to the Father's heart, who has made him known." The flesh of Jesus Christ, his humanity, is the necessary corridor into the Father's presence. His Crib and his Cross lead to his glory. The more surely we grasp by faith his abasement, the more transparent this becomes, allowing his glory to shine through, until finally the complete unveiling of his light is accomplished, whereby abasement is transformed into glory and flesh becomes *logos, kyrios, pneuma* (Word, Lord, Spirit). Whoever rejects Christ's flesh rejects also the *logos*; whoever despises Christ's humanity despises also his divinity; but whoever humbly inclines towards Jesus' humanity, ready to share his reproach, sees the *logos* in the flesh of Jesus. The flesh is then no longer means and way but life and reality.

And so it is perfectly true that the glory of Christ can be seen in the helpless Child in the Crib, and that in him we see the light of God. Concerning the shepherds of Bethlehem, Ambrose wrote: "They hurry along to look upon the *logos*; for when we look upon the flesh of the Lord we look upon the *logos*, and he is the Son."(1) It is precisely in weakness that God's power is revealed:

> For this reason Jesus became weak for the sake of the weak in order to ransom them; I have become all things to all men.... He was wounded for our sins and became weak on account of our iniquities. He became a child, an infant at the breast, so that you could become a perfect man; he was wrapped in swaddling bands so that you could be disentangled from the snares of death; he lay in a crib so that you could stand at the altar; he came down to earth to raise you to the stars; he found no room at the inn so that you could inhabit a many-mansioned heaven. He was rich and became poor for your sake, so that his poverty might endow you with wealth. The Lord's poverty is my wealth and his weakness my strength. He preferred to become poor himself so as to be rich for all mankind. The tears of that weeping infant have washed me; those tears have washed my sins away. Lord Jesus, I owe more to your indignity, which redeemed me, than to your might which created me. What use would have been my creation, had I never been redeemed!(2)

This is the economy of the flesh, in which is revealed the *agape* of God, which exceeds all human glory. Ambrose continues:

The whole form of divinity, however, can never be contained in a body. The form of the flesh is one thing, the glory of God quite another. It is for your sake that he is weak, intrinsically he is power. For your sake he is poor, intrinsically he is rich. Do not regard only what you see, but recognize that you have been redeemed. With your eyes you see him wrapped in swaddling bands; but you do not see that he lives in heaven.... He was born out of the womb, but he shines in heaven. He lies in an earthly inn, but he is aglow with heavenly light. He was born of a married woman, but conceived by a virgin....(3)

If you are not to judge yourself by human standards but by Christ, how much more ought you to measure Christ not in human terms, but on his own terms.(4)

We must not therefore remain with the things of the flesh. We must travel along the road of the flesh with Jesus, so that through the humility of the flesh we may rise up to the glory of *agape*. The two belong together in Christ and also in us. The star of faith must lead us to the Crib; but in the Infant we must adore God. As gifts we bring him ourselves, so that he may divinize us. The person who sees and comprehends the Cross in the Epiphany is led to glory by the Lord himself. "Father, you revealed your Son to the nations by the guidance of a star. Lead us to your glory in heaven by the light of faith" (*Collect for the Epiphany*).

5
The Epiphany of our Lord

Jesus, our way to God

Comparing today's feast with Christmas, the first thing that strikes us is that we have moved out of deep silence and obscurity into a world of noise and bustle. At Christmas all nature holds its breath. The peace and tranquillity of eternity spreads over all the earth. The liturgy proclaims: "When peaceful silence lay over all, and night had run half of her swift course, your all-powerful word, O Lord, leaped down from heaven, from the royal throne." God's Word is heard issuing out of eternal silence. Only the angels make audible jubilation, and that too speaks of peace on earth. On today's feast things are different: there comes the grand entrance of our ruler, the *adventus*, with all its pomp and circumstance, as was enacted in the ancient Orient and in the Hellenic kingdoms and also in times of Roman rule, on the entrance of the emperor. For the ancients such an arrival was a revelation of divinity, a making visible of the power and glory of the divine. "Lordliness," which is the Germanic form of the word "glory," is still redolent of the splendor that surrounded the advent of the Lord. *Kyrios* and glory belong together; in the *Te Deum* we still acclaim Christ as *rex gloriae*, the King of Glory. The Old Testament was already painting a picture of the coming of God, in all the brilliant colors that were at hand in ancient oriental idiom.

The sacred liturgy has collected these texts for us and applied them to Christ. From this source has emerged the richness and color of the liturgy of this feast. The Introit is indeed an entrance song for an emperor, re-echoing the fanfares of a warlike people and the acclamations of the crowds. "Behold, he comes—the Lord, the Ruler; in his hand are royalty, power and empire." The citizens shouted: "*regnum*—royalty"; the officials shouted: "*potestas*—power"; the soldiers shouted: "*imperium*—imperial might". In the Gospel we are shown how from the far east and from the ends of the earth, wise men, priests, and kings come bringing their tribute and offering homage. There is an air of universality about the responsorial psalm: kings come from Tarshish in the farthest west and from distant Arabia in the east to venerate their great king; and all nations bow before his rule.

On today's feast it is Jerusalem, the king's city, and not the peaceful countryside of the shepherds, that is honored by the royal entry. Today the city beholds its king, and with him comes his bride, the empress, who with her retinue follows behind the king, and is about to marry him during the festival of his accession to the throne. He has already prepared the bridal bath, into which he descends before her and in which he purifies her so that she will be a worthy consort in his kingdom. His coming is from all eternity: "Royal dignity was yours...from the dawn of your earliest days" (Ps 110). Today his radiance flows over the whole congregation of God, upon the city set upon a hill. Through him it has become filled with sheer delight, because his glory has shone upon it. Towards this city, from out of the world's darkness, now stream in its sons and daughters, hitherto scattered, but now united in one kingdom. All the glory of the world now converges upon one place, upon the royal palace of the ruler of the aeons, who now rules from his throne and bestows gifts upon his servants and upon his sons and daughters.

When holy mother Church on this feast day paints for us a picture of this magical world, that surpasses all fairy-tale wonders, she proves herself the most gifted of poets; and because what she depicts is no mere fantasy, but reality, she proves herself to be a prophet. In Numbers 24 it was said of the prophet, "The spirit of God came upon him...the oracle of the man with far-seeing eyes...of one who hears the word of God...sees what Shaddai makes him see...receives the divine answer, and his eyes are opened."

On this feast day this is how the Church, the Bride, views the beauty, the wealth and might of her Bridegroom, the King's Son, who has chosen her. This is no mere outward, materialistic show. All of the images she uses are symbols of the pneumatic, divine reality which unveils itself to her spiritual sight. Christ appears to her. It is true that first of all he has appeared in outward, human form. But this appearing goes far beyond the *natus est* of Christmas. In terms of outward appearance what appears today is not much more than could be seen at Nazareth—a little boy on his mother's lap, dwelling in a little house in modest poverty. It is true that strange men approach the Child, offering him rich gifts, and in this event a new radiance begins to shine; but it soon dims and we see a poor carpenter, who flees with his wife and baby by night in the mist to a foreign land.

Thus the *appearing* signifies something quite different. It is a *divine, pneumatic* light that shines out, revealing to the Church the glory of what appears. It is no earthly glitter and show that is signified by these oriental, fairy-tale splendors, but rather the splendor of God, appearing in the Child of Bethlehem. "The Lord is God, he smiles on us" (Ps 118:27). "Arise, shine out, for your light has come, the glory of the Lord is rising on you.... Above you the Lord now rises and above you his glory appears" (Is 60:1f.).

Today's feast is by no means an externalizing of the Christmas revelation, is no secularizing of the spirituality of Nazareth. On the contrary it is an interiorizing and spiritualizing of the feast of Christmas and its mystery. Today for the first time we become wholly concerned about who he is of whom we sing: "A Child is born to us, to us a Son is given." The shepherds saw the Child in the Crib and adored him as the Redeemer, the Messiah. The magi paid him homage as king of the Jews. Today the Church probes deeper into the mystery—"O God, today you have made known your only-begotten Son to the pagans." They too see the Child and adore him, embracing him with all the devotion of humble love. But they see more than the form of an infant. They look deeper and see the only-begotten of the Father; they already see him as at the Jordan, when he was acknowledged by the Father and the Holy Spirit. "This is my beloved Son" (Lk 3:22). They are seeing him as when "he revealed his glory" (Jn 2:11) in signs and wonders. For them he is a true unveiling of "the message which was a mystery hidden for generations" (Col 1:26). Today they proclaim: "The Word was made flesh, he lived among us, and we saw his glory, the glory that is his as the only Son of the Father, full of grace and truth" (Jn 1:14).

The revelation of divinity does not, however, detract from the reality and truth, from the starkly physical facts that the Christmas Gospel records. The poverty of the Crib and the reality of a child of flesh and blood are not dimmed or diminished. On the contrary all of these things are confirmed, and they in their turn become a corroboration of God's revelation. It is precisely here that we discover the Christian miracle; we perceive what is distinctive and truly divine about the reality of Christ, that in this event the earthly and the heavenly, the flesh and the spirit, humanity and divinity, have become one. "The Word became flesh and we saw his glory." If we human beings were to have thought out a revelation of God, we would have conceived vast philosophical systems, would have allowed mighty shafts of light to stream into our minds out of the highest heavens, would have racked our brains in speculation, and only the most learned could have hoped to see a glimmer of the light of truth. God does things in a quite different manner. He begins neither with words of wisdom and philosophy nor with universities and professorial chairs. His revelation begins with a tiny infant and ends on the Cross.

After the death of the French philosopher Pascal, there was found, sewn into the lining of his coat, a little parchment and a sheet of paper. Both contained the record of a spiritual experience which Pascal had in the year 1654. This striking document begins thus:

> Fire, the God of Abraham, of Isaac, and of Jacob,
> not the God of the philosophers and scholars,
> certainty, certainty, feeling, joy, peace.
> God Jesus Christ...
> he will be found only in the ways
> that are taught in the Gospel...
> Jesus Christ,
> Jesus Christ.

Long before Pascal, the Church had recognized the same thing in her mysteries. The only way that leads to God is the way through Jesus Christ the man, the baby in the Crib, the man upon the Cross. All other ways, be they never so exalted, are blind alleys and lead away from God. On the other hand, whoever follows the way of the Incarnation, is led by God along the way of divinization.

This is what today's feast teaches. It displays to us the one lying in a manger as the *God-logos*, who alone is the genuine image of the eternal Father, in whom we see the Father himself. This Child is God's Son, the *logos* of God, the truth and Wisdom of God—he is God.

We will never be able to fathom these depths. We can, however, say this: had God been only truth and wisdom and being, he might well have revealed himself in a way that would have been more agreeable to the philosophers. But his real essence is *agape*—love. *Agape* is so infinitely deep, so broad, so high and so long, that it could be revealed only in the Child and in the Crucified. "What proves that God loves us is that Christ died for us while we were still sinners" (Rom 5:8). John expresses it this way: "God's love for us was revealed when God sent into the world his only Son so that we could have life through him; this is the love I mean: not our love for God, but God's love for us when he sent his Son to be the sacrifice that takes our sins away" (1 Jn 4:9f.).

If *agape* is the essence of God, the Epiphany of the Son is the supreme revelation of God, and along the road of *agape* we press on to the *gnosis* (knowledge) of God. More and more we recognize that the Child of Nazareth is the God who has become visible to us. He is the Son of the Father, a Person distinct from the Father. The Father dwells in unapproachable light; the Son manifests himself. And yet, the Son is one with the Father, so that we see the Father in the incarnate Son. With the Son, in the Son and through the Son, we penetrate the ultimate principle, the Father himself, and behold in blissful vision the unity of the Father and the Son and the Holy Spirit.

Today's feast teaches us to look upon, and believe in, the divine Personhood of the Son, and at the same time to acknowledge the unity within the Blessed Trinity. It shows us the condescension of the divine *agape* even to accepting the shame of the manger and the Cross; and it shows us also its exaltation, through which we are raised up to share in the life of the true God, who is for ever enthroned in heaven. At no time have the pagans been able to grasp this mystery. In the second century Celsus, an adversary of the Christians, wrote: "Were they to worship only one God, their doctrines might have some substance beside others; but they worship this Jesus, who has recently appeared, with excessive devotion and believe that they do not offend God when they thus venerate his servants."(1) Origen answered him in this manner:

If Celsus had only understood the saying, "I and the Father are one," he would not then have thought that we worship anyone other than the one God, who is exalted above all things. The truth is: "the Father is in me and I am in the Father."...We worship the Father and the Son as one God...for we believe him who said... "Before Abraham was, I am" and "I am the truth," and none of us is so foolish as to believe, that there was no truth before the Epiphany of Christ. And so we worship the Father of truth and the Son as the truth, two beings in respect of their substance, but one in respect of unity of will. Whoever has seen the Son, who is the reflection of the eternal light and pure emanation of the glory of the Almighty, has seen in him, God himself.(2)

To be able to celebrate this feast day as a genuine mystery, one must have arrived at a sound perception of faith and an adequate vision of faith. One must have been able to see in the Child whom the magi adored the Son of the eternal Father of *agape*, and so have attained to a vision of the Father himself. In this vision he will already have found blessedness. "They were overwhelmed with joy" (Mt 2:11). Full of this joy the magi presented their gifts. And we too like them offer our gifts in the joy of *agape*: the gold of true faith, the incense of sacrificial prayer, the myrrh of patience and love of the Cross, but also our indestructible belief in the Resurrection, which the God whom we now see has given us. "Now that his glory has shone among us you have renewed humanity in his immortal image" (*Preface of the Epiphany*).

6
Good Friday

Authentic adoration of the Cross

Is THE HOMAGE, the adoration, we offer to the Cross justified? Ought we, who are supposed to adore God alone, offer any such veneration to the Cross? We hear voices raised, even from very early times, against any adoration of the Cross. In the third century Minucius Felix told the pagans: "We neither adore the Cross nor wish to do so." He continued: "You pagans, indeed, who hew your gods out of wood, may perhaps worship wooden crosses as parts of your gods. What then are the emblems and banners of your soldiers if not gilded and adorned crosses? Indeed, your victory signs do not merely copy the form of the cross, but the form of the man nailed upon it as well...."(1)

This early Christian apologist saw something pagan in the adoration of the Cross, and so rejected it. Did Christians then later on imitate pagan customs and begin to adore the Cross? By no means. Nonetheless the comparison with pagan idolatry warns us that the *adoratio crucis* must be properly conceived. It is not enough to venerate the holy Cross, to kiss it, to adore it and so to promise oneself salvation by means of this external worship. That would be a regression into heathendom. Christians must venerate the Cross in a way totally different from the way that pagans venerate their idols; we dare not worship mere wood. It is not the wood but Christ who is exalted in this sign, in this banner. We venerate the Cross as a symbol, as a mystery-sign that points towards the mystery of salvation. Christ himself, nailed to the Cross, who on the Cross became the Cross, Christ the High Priest with outstretched hands, he it is whom we venerate and adore in the Cross. In the sign, too, that will be seen in the heavens when our Lord comes to judge, the early Christians did not see the Cross but the Lord himself, in the form of a Cross. In the *Didache* (16:6), one of our oldest documents (beginning of the second century), we read: "Then (that is, at the *parousia*) the sign of truth will appear, first the sign of spreading out in heaven." This has been interpreted to mean "the spreading out of the hands." Christ will appear with hands extended, not in pain as once upon the Cross, but in victory, embracing the whole world and drawing it to himself.

When we venerate and adore the holy Cross, it is Jesus the Lord whom we venerate, adoring him who has won victory through this Cross, and who through this victory has turned the sign of humiliation and death into a symbol and mystery of life and glory. We ought not to think of Christ as the one who was crucified and then in addition happened to be exalted in glory, as though his glorification came after his humiliation. The Crucified *as such* is the glorified one; the Cross did not become the sign of glory only after the Resurrection, but is itself essentially the sign of glory. The sign of the Cross is a recapitulation in a single sign of all that we venerate, love, and adore in Christ our Savior, and we thank God for that sign through all eternity.

What power this sign possesses, being able both to reveal and at the same time to veil such a wealth of the most sublime reality! In the Cross the mystery of God is made visible, but veiled from our sight; only the eye of faith can perceive the inner reality of the Cross. Unbelief sees nothing. The unbeliever may indeed sense something of the power of this sign. That is why he detests it with diabolical rage and is forced to retreat from it.

Commenting on Psalm 119:107, "O Lord, though my suffering is acute, revive me as your word has guaranteed," St Hilary wrote:

> When the devil dared to tempt the Lord, he boasted that the world belonged to him. But the Lord commands us to die to the world so as to live for him. Living with the Lord, contempt of riches becomes our wealth, contempt of worldly honors our inheriting the kingdom of heaven; living with the Lord, abasement of the heart becomes the badge of noble and royal birth. Christ wanted us to learn from him the greatest of all virtues. The Apostle, too, admonishes us to practice humility. "In your minds you must be the same as Christ Jesus: his state was divine, yet he did not cling to his equality with God but emptied himself to assume the condition of a slave, and became as men are; and being as all men are, he was humbler yet, even to accepting death, death on a cross" [Phil 2:5-8]. In this we are shown the only-begotten Son of God himself as our model of humility. But we must note also the distinction that accompanies this abasement: "But God raised him high and gave him the name which is above all other names so that all beings in the heavens, on the earth and in the underworld, should bend the knee at the name of Jesus and that every tongue should acclaim Jesus Christ as Lord, to the glory of God the Father" [Phil 2:9-11]. This was the reward he received in return for his abasement: his body was taken up and now lives in the glory of the Father, so that all beings in heaven, on earth and in the underworld bow the knee to him. Because he always was substantially in the Godhead, he never considered that there was any need for him to grasp for himself through force or theft that which was already his, viz. divinity. He was one in substance with God, and lacked none of the glory of him in whose being he rested. In his abasement he took upon himself the form of a slave, in outward appearance being seen as a man; and through obedience he humbled himself to accepting death—more than that, death on a cross. And it is

he who at God's command established the heavens, equipped the cosmos with all its solidity and beauty, who created the earth and all that is upon the earth. But was it all of those accomplishments that qualified him to introduce the humanity he assumed into the glory of the eternal Father? No,—that was the prize for his self-emptying, that the reward for his humility. Although he remained always in God, yet he came into time and took on himself the form of a slave, and so, both in the form of God and of slave, he is recognized as the one whom all the powers of heaven, of earth, and of the underworld acclaim, that he is in the glory of God the Father.(2)

What a wonderful mystery of God is thus revealed to us! Even the glory of the Son of God, insofar as he is man, derives not from his exalted, divine pedigree, nor from his mighty deeds, but from his humility and abasement. This truly is a hidden mystery that can be unveiled to human beings only by God. Men, even virtuous men, expect to see glory in dignity and splendor or in mighty achievements, in words or works that make a huge impact upon the world. God, on the other hand, exalted his Son by debasing him. The humiliated God-man rose up above all the powers that are to become the *kyrios*, before whom every knee bends and whom every tongue confesses: "Jesus the Lord" (1 Cor 12:3), and "Jesus is Lord in the glory of God the Father" (Phil 2:11). Now as man he sits enthroned beside the Father, and shares in the Father's glory. The supreme, hidden glory of the Father, the glory that is beyond the power of human eye to see, or of human action to approach, has been conferred upon him who, in deepest humility, stripped himself of all glory so as to show perfect obedience to the Father.

Here we touch upon a mystery that exceeds the grasp of our intellect. Faith alone is able to penetrate such mysteries and gain, from a distance, some notion of their meaning. Again we quote St Hilary of Poitiers on Psalm 139.

These things are not hidden from us, but they are to the wise of this world. The Apostle bears witness that all of the Church's mysteries give hope in a veiled manner, when he writes: "If you read my words you will have some idea of the depths that I see in the mystery of Christ. This mystery that has now been revealed through the Spirit to his holy apostles and prophets was unknown to any men in past generations; it means that pagans now share the same inheritance, that they are parts of the same body, and that the same promise has been made to them, in Christ Jesus through the gospel" (Eph 3:4ff.). In another place he writes; "I became the servant of the Church when God made me responsible for delivering God's message to you, the message which was a mystery hidden for generations and centuries and has now been revealed to his saints. ...The mystery is Christ among you, your hope of glory" (Col 1:25ff.). The mystery of "Christ in us" had been hidden, but now the Father has lifted the veil. To Peter it was said: "It was not flesh and blood that revealed this to you but my Father in heaven" (Mt 16;17). And so it has been disclosed that Christ is in us, in the poor in spirit, in the sorrowful, in the lowly ones of this earth, in the off-scourings of society, in the last within the Church. The last in the Church—these are those bowed down by whatever manner of abasement. This hidden mystery has been unveiled and it is: 'God in us'.(3)

Just as Christ was raised to glory in the Father through his humiliation, so those who are "in Christ" can be exalted in no other way except through the abasement of the Cross; for the new life, lived by those who sit with the Son and hence with the Father, so far surpasses all earthly life that it can be reached only through death. The Lord said to Peter: "It was not flesh and blood that revealed this to you but my Father in heaven" (Mt 16:17). St Paul teaches the very same thing: "Flesh and blood cannot inherit the kingdom of God "(1 Cor 15:50). All that is this-worldly must vanish, all the pride of life must die, every earthly aspiration must be trodden underfoot, if true life is to be won. For this reason Jesus was obedient; he surrendered his natural desire to live, he threw away all self-assertion. He was obedient even to death, offering the very last thing anyone has to give, that is his ego, which wants to preserve at least its existence. Yes, he was obedient even to death on the Cross, ready to suffer the ultimate indignity of losing the freedom to end his life in peace. He found himself an outcast from the human race, hanging between heaven and earth, condemned as a criminal, his life violently snuffed out. And so nothing was left of his earthly being; he was truly *exinanitus*—totally emptied. In the very moment, however, that he became dead to this world he began to live for God. For the first time now as man he was the true Son, the eternal Son, who sits at the Father's right hand and shares in his being, sunk deep in the life of the Father, of whom it is said: "*apud te est fons vitae*—with you is the fountain of life"(Ps 36:9).

It is now plain to see that the decisive event in the life of Jesus was his death. From time to time one hears it said today that there are two ways of walking with the Lord. We may accompany him on his earthly journeys or venerate him as the exalted one. Both ways are said to be good, and each Christian must choose the way that suits him. This view is not in harmony with the scriptures or the teaching of the Fathers. Holy scripture demonstrates clearly how the Lord himself throughout his life constantly alluded to his death: "Now we are going up to Jerusalem" (Lk 18:31). His whole life on earth was one offertory procession towards the hour of his death, which then became his entry into the Father's presence.

St John, who saw Jesus already radiant in the light of glory, says none the less that the Lord would be glorified in his sacrificial death. According to St John, on the eve of his Passion the Lord prayed: "Father, glorify your Son" (Jn 17:1). His glorification comes only through his Passion. "Was it not ordained that the Christ should suffer and so enter into his glory," Jesus explained to the two disciples after his resurrection (Lk 24:26). This is the mysterious law of Christian perfection. Perfection is attained only through death, through the Cross. The life of God is so infinitely precious, so unfathomably deep, that it can be bought only at the cost of giving up all that is earthly. Anyone who is not prepared to abandon life cannot gain life. This applies to all earthly and temporal things. Even in the worldly sphere all greatness or eminence demands total dedication. How much more does possession of the eternal inheritance that is God himself demand consecration to the point of death.

Let us not, therefore, venerate the Cross with mere outward show of singing, praying and kissing; let us venerate it, rather, by imitating our Savior who is the Cross. Let us be willing to offer whatever sacrifice life demands of us, for "the troubles which are soon over, though they weigh little, train us for the carrying of a weight of eternal glory which is out of all proportion to them. And so we have no eyes for things that are visible, but only for things that are invisible; for visible things last only for a time, and the invisible things are eternal" (2 Cor 4:17f.).

7
Easter

The Lord's Pasch—passing over into new life

THE PASCH OF the Lord, the Pasch, and again I say the Pasch to the glory of the Blessed Trinity. For us this is the feast of feasts, the celebration of celebrations, related not so much to things on this earth as to Christ himself, whom it celebrates. This feast outshines all others as the sun outshines all of the stars."(1) This voice from Christian antiquity demonstrates to us what Easter meant to the Christians of the east, even though by the fourth century a whole series of other festivals, notably the incarnation feasts of Christmas and Epiphany had been instituted. Later, new feasts were constantly being added; but even today this whole bright constellation is unable to dim the radiance of the Easter Sun. The Pasch is still *the* festival of the Christian.

What is a feast? A feast is a celebration by a community in which it recognizes its own innermost essence and through which, out of the communal awareness of its life, it gains increased impetus to its life. There are feasts of nature and feasts of the community. In nature-feasts men and women experience the recurrent new blooming of the power of natural life; in community-feasts those who have assembled together become aware of the powers that brought them together and upon which their continued existence depends. Alongside the life of nature and of humankind there is an infinitely higher life—the life of the Godhead. Even the heathen sought to drink in this divine life and so celebrated their feasts. In his own strength the heathen was unable to rise above the powers which rule over the cosmos. To puny man these powers appeared as gods.

Through Christ alone did it become possible for us to gain access to the life of the true God, who has been and is for ever, and who is hidden from our sight. We read in John 3:13: "No one has gone up to heaven except the one who came down from heaven." And in John 1:18 we read: "No one has ever seen God; it is the only Son, who is nearest to the Father's heart, who has made him known." God became man in order to bring to us the life of God. "The Word was made flesh, he lived among us, and we saw his glory, the glory that is his as the only Son of the Father, full of grace and truth" (Jn 1:14). "All that came to be had life in him and that life was the light of men..." (Jn 1:4). Only he who is life can bring life to men. And so for us the appearing of God in the flesh is the subject of a very great feast, because through the God who has become flesh, the divine life has become accessible to us. Ought we then to celebrate only his Epiphany? To do so would be consonant neither with scripture nor with the history of mankind nor with our own experience.

One of the most fundamental things about men and women is their sense of guilt in the divine presence. The mythologies of all nations tell of the sinfulness of the human race, and the record of sacred scripture confirms that in the beginning our first parents sinned of their own free will, and turned away from eternal Love to indulge their pride. For this reason God could not give us a direct vision of his glory. Instead, the incarnate God took upon himself "sinful flesh" (Rm 8:3). He, the eternally pure One, bore the weight of our guilt so as to free us from sin and save us from death and hell. New life could spring up only out of the death of sinful man. And so it is not the Epiphany but the Cross of our Lord Jesus Christ that has become the subject of the authentic and sole feast of Christians.

God, the infinitely merciful and just, gave up his own Son to suffer death on the Cross, so as to fulfill all righteousness and demonstrate his infinite mercy. "What proves that God loves us is that Christ died for us while we were still sinners" (Rm 5:8). In Philippians 2:5ff. Paul admonishes us to adopt the same mind as was in Christ who did not cling to his divine prestige, although he was one in substance with God, but emptied himself and became obedient to death on the Cross. And in the very moment he died on the Cross, in the deepest abasement and showing perfect loving obedience to the Father, sin was expiated and our primeval guilt removed. From the baptismal fire of the Cross the new, eternally transfigured man arose—the Lord Jesus Christ, before whom every knee in heaven and on earth and in the underworld bends, proclaiming him Lord, in the glory of the Father. This is the greatest transformation that the world has ever seen—from the deepest humiliation, from the depths of sin's misery to supreme exaltation at God's right hand. He who had hung upon the Cross as a condemned criminal now reigns in eternal majesty at the Father's right hand as king of mankind, waiting until all his enemies are desroyed and he assumes his rule over all things.

That which has happened to the Head has happened to the whole Body. From the whole span of world history the Lord assembles his members, until his Body is complete and ripe for entry into the everlasting kingdom of God. But each individual Christian must re-live in his own life, that which the Lord has lived through first. The Christian cannot, it is true, in his own strength carry the cross of this life victoriously, but he can carry it in virtue of his victorious captain—"the leader who would take them to their salvation"(Heb 2:10). The road along which the Christian must share in the sufferings of his leader is, however, the road of faith, and in faith he must play his part in the mysteries of Christ. The Lord was not content simply to accomplish his redemptive act once and for all, but wanted this act to be accessible to all the faithful down the centuries. And so he inserted his salvific action into the Church's mysteries, so that it would be operative there until the end of time, and so that each one of the faithful could emulate his action and win thereby the fruits of redemption. Leo the Great wrote: "That which was made visible in the Lord flowed over into the mysteries."(2)

And so we come to the holy season of the Pasch. The Pasch is nothing other than the annual making present in the Church of the redemptive work of the Lord, the work that he accomplished through his death and resurrection. It is, therefore, not just the recalling to mind of events that occurred almost 2000 years ago, but rather the making these events present for us in the sacramental realities. By faith and through the sacred liturgy we enter into the very redemptive act of our Lord himself and, as his members, take part in the action of our Head. Only because this is so can the Church look forward to, and then celebrate, the holy Pasch with such lively excitement. In chapter 49 of his Rule St Benedict wrote that the monks ought "to look forward to the celebration of the holy Pasch with spiritual joy." Today there streams out from the Pasch, as from our Lord himself, all of the life and salvation that is in the Church. This is reason enough for our celebrating feasts and throwing ourselves into them with the deepest spiritual joy. And all the other feasts draw their power from this one feast of Christendom, from the ultimate source of all supernatural life in the Church.

In the earliest days the Church understood the Pasch as the sacred "passing over" which Christ along with his Church had accomplished, a passing through death into eternal life. "Pasch" does indeed mean "passing over" and originally it denoted death's angel passing by the houses of the Israelites, who had sprinkled their door-posts with the blood of the lamb. In this word the Fathers of the Church saw an allusion to the passing over from the aeon of sin and death into the aeon of

Christ and of eternal life. In the word many of the Greek Fathers sensed an echo of the Greek word *paschein* meaning "to suffer" and so they equated "Pasch" with "Passion." At all events, for early Christians "Pasch" was not the name given to the Easter feast proper, but to the time of preparation, including above all the passion of our Lord. In the strict sense the Pasch is the dividing line between death and life, in other words a transition from mourning to joy as is celebrated in the Easter Vigil. Therefore it was preceded by a fast which even in the earliest times lasted forty hours, running from the hour of our Lord's death until his resurrection. This was the fast of which our Lord himself had spoken when he said that the friends of the Bridegroom would fast when the bridegroom was taken from them (Mk 2:19f.). During this fast one tried to enter into the feelings of the disciples when they saw their beloved master and Lord being violently torn from them and sent to the most gruesome of deaths. This was the collapse of their entire world; they lost their heads and rushed hither and thither, Peter going so far as to deny his Lord.

When the Lord died on the Cross the whole world was thrown into darkness; the darkness which had been overcome by the light of creation seemed to have returned. We can understand, therefore, why year by year, in imitation of the apostles, the Church gives herself over to the deepest mourning and complaint in these days before the Pasch, using the so-called "Lamentations" from the prophet Jeremiah in the liturgy of Matins on Good Friday. The Church does know that chaos will not reign permanently and that the sun will rise again. Even so, in these days she abandons herself to fasting and penance, because she is still living in this world of sin and is still threatened on all sides by the danger of death. Unlike Judas, however, she does not give way to despair, but trusts in the love that has revealed itself on the Cross. Her mourning is shot through with hope. In these days the Church gives herself up to prayer and scripture-reading, because therein she sees the light of Christ shining, and because in the archetypes of scripture she detects the prefiguring of the passion and victory of her Bridegroom. By the light of prophecy she learns that the Lord, who out of *agape* took all this upon himself will not remain in death, but will impart his life to her.

In this mood she enters this holiest of nights, this great Easter Vigil when, according to the rules of the ancient Church, no one dared sleep, but stayed awake in order to go out with lamps lit to greet the Bridegroom when he comes. Of old the Church believed that it would be during the Easter Vigil that he would return. If by midnight he had not returned, they joyfully ended the fast by celebrating the holy eucharist. In this meal the Lord came to them, not in manifest glory, but in a mystery. In their midst he performed his mighty act of redemption, revealing his glorious resurrection from the dead and, through the new covenant in his body and blood, giving all a share in his eternal life with the Father. Then by the power of the Saviour appearing in glory, virgin mother Church, who had emerged from the water and blood flowing from the Saviour's side, brought forth for her Bridegroom new children out of the font—a new generation born to enjoy eternal life. These new children received the fullness of the new life through the mystery of the Spirit, through confirmation, and for the first time were permitted to pray along with the faithful and refresh themselves with the bread and wine of eternal life. In addition they were given a beaker with milk and honey, signifying that they were now living in the promised land of God. In this manner the Church entered into the sacred transition that is the Pasch, and passed over from the world of sin and death into the bright kingdom of Christ, into the life of eternity, wich begins while we are still on this earth, but reaches it summit only when the Lord comes again.

8
The Easter Season

Pentecost—the symbol of completion

THE SACRED PASCH as understood in the oldest Christian liturgy, that is in the Easter Vigil, is a *transition*—"it is a passover in honor of Yahweh" (Ex 12:11). According to the original Hebrew text it was the passing over of the angel of the Lord, who passed by the blood-sprinkled door-posts of the Israelites, but slew the first-born of the Egyptians. Although it was this passing over that gave the name to the Jewish feast of the Pasch, the Pasch denoted the passing out of the land of slavery in Egypt into the Promised Land of freedom and of the Covenant. John the Evangelist gave a New Testament meaning to the word when he wrote: "It was before the festival of the Passover, and Jesus knew that the hour had come for him to pass from this world to the Father. He had always loved those who were his in the world, but now he showed how perfect his love was" (Jn 13:1). For Christians, therefore, the Pasch is the passing out of this world, out of this aeon, out of this place of darkness and sin into the presence and life of the Father, first of the Lord himself, and then of all his disciples. This means that the Cross is the Pasch. The Cross is the great parting of the ways that looks in two dirtections: towards the mortification of sinful flesh and towards the triumph of supernatural life. The goal of the passing over is life with the Father. Paul expresses this in another way: "Christ, as we know, having been raised from the dead will never die again. Death has no power over him any more. When he died, he died, once for all, to sin, so his life now is life with God" (Rm 6:9f.). The phrase "once for all" denotes the crossing of the boundary of this Pasch, passing out of the realm of sin through death into true life. The Pasch, so conceived, is thus the great entrance-gate into life with God. Christ is our leader and our model, our signpost and also the source of our strength. "You too must consider yourselves to be dead to sin but alive for God in Christ Jesus" (Rm 6:11). The Lord's Pasch becomes our Pasch, and the eternal life enjoyed by our Lord with the Father becomes our life. Through faith we enter into the mysteries of Christ, and through participation in these we enjoy, as members of Christ, a share in all that Christ suffered on our behalf. In his Easter sermon St Gaudens of Brescia said:

> If I call Easter the birthday of the new-born world, I mean that it is our birthday, for we who formerly lived for sin and were dead to righteousness have been born again in Christ. Now we have died to the evil of our former sins and live for God, because we have been conformed to the death and to the resurrection of Christ. In baptism we were buried with him in death so that as Christ rose from the dead we could walk in new life with him, celebrating the feast and glorifying the Cross of the Lord Jesus Christ.

Our new life of holiness and righteousness is built upon the grace of the Lord, upon our sharing in the life of the transfigured one; this is a righteousness we have not acquired by our own merit, for it is a gift of God's grace, which nonetheless lives effectively in us. This new life of Christ in us is a sheer gift of God and yet it is our own possession. "Get rid of the old yeast, and make yourselves into a completely new batch of bread, unleavened as you are meant to be. Christ, our passover, has been sacrificed; let us celebrate the feast, then, by getting rid of all the old yeast of evil and wickedness, having only the unleavened bread of sincerity and truth" (1 Cor 5f.).

These few texts are sufficient to explain already what *Pentecost* is. If the Pasch is the passing out of this aeon into the one to come, if the Cross is the death of the life of sin and of death itself, Pentecost, which immediately blossoms out of this, is *life in* God, life in the new, eternal aeon of Christ, in the purity and righteousness of God. Through the gate of the Pasch we come into the Christian feast, the feast of the exaltation of the Lord, of which Paul wrote that God raised him, who had been humiliated in his obedience, and "gave him the name which is above all names so that all beings in the heavens, on earth and in the underworld should bend the knee at the name of Jesus and that every tongue should acclaim that Jesus Christ is Lord, to the glory of God the Father" (Phil 2:9ff.). Jesus' new name is *kyrios*, which signifies that Jesus, even in his human nature shared in the manifest glory of God; that is, Jesus, who hitherto had hidden his glory as the Son of God, is now in his humanity the king of all creation, and sits in his glorified flesh enthroned at the right hand of the divine majesty on high. *Qui crucifixus erat, Deus ecce per omnia regnat* (Venantius Fortunatus). Pentecost—the fifty day period between the Pasch and the descent of the Holy Spirit—was regarded by the early Church as an Easter festival. Soon Easter Sunday began to be called the Pasch; but the basic idea of the primitive Pentecost is still with us, for it is founded upon scripture and the tradition of the Church.

Scripture and tradition know of two ways in which our Lord's redemptive acts can be regarded and correspondingly celebrated. Both ways are essentially Christian and are complementary. The first way inclines towards the metaphysical and spiritual; it surveys God's eternal plan of salvation in a single glance. In the New Testament this way is followed principally by St Paul and St John. The other way regards rather the historical sequence of redemptive events, looking at them more from the human perspective—Luke is a good example. We are accustomed today to contemplate and celebrate first of all the passion of our Lord and then his resurrection; forty days later we celebrate his ascension and finally, on the fiftieth day, we celebrate the descent of the Holy Spirit. In the earliest days the Church took all of this in at a single glance. St John's approach can help us today to gain a deeper understanding of Pentecost, and so of the feast of Easter; he lets us see the mystery of redemption in its grand unity, as it was conceived from all eternity in the mind of God, and how it then gradually unfolded and was consummated in time.

Paul wrote to the Ephesians: "When he ascended to the height, he captured prisoners, he gave gifts to men. When it says 'he ascended', what can it mean if not that he descended right down to the lower regions of the earth? The one who rose higher than all the heavens to fill all things is none other than the one who descended" (Eph 4:8-10).

At one glance this letter takes in the whole redemptive work of Christ: our High Priest with his own blood enters the heavenly sanctuary; there he stands, our Mediator.

St John tells us that Jesus cried out on the great last day of the festival of Tabernacles: "If any man is thirsty, let him come to me! Let the man come and drink who believes in me!" (Jn 7:37-39). The evangelist interprets this as the fulfillment of the prophetic word: "From his breast shall flow fountains of living water. He was speaking of the Spirit which those who believed in him were to receive; for there was no Spirit as yet because Jesus had not yet been glorified." Later John identifies the glorification of Jesus with his journey through his passion (12:28ff.). At his entry into Jerusalem our Lord prayed to the Father:

"Father, glorify your name!" A voice came from heaven, "I have glorified it, and I will glorify it again..." Jesus answered, "It was not for my sake this voice came, but for yours. Now is sentence being passed on this world; now the prince of this world is to be overthrown. And when I am lifted up from the earth, I shall draw all men to myself." By these words he indicated the kind of death he would die (Jn 12:28ff.).

When Judas went out to betray his master, Jesus said: "Now has the Son of Man been glorified, and in him God has been glorified. If God has been glorified in him, God will in turn glorify him in himself, and will glorify him very soon" (Jn 13:31f.). In his last prayer in the presence of the disciples, Jesus said: "Father, the hour has come: glorify your Son so that your Son may glorify you" (Jn 17:1). After these prophetic words had been fufilled, John records the words the risen Lord spoke to Mary of Magdala: "Do not cling to me, because I have not yet ascended to my Father. But go and find the brothers, and tell them I am ascending to my Father and your Father, to my God and your God" (Jn 20:17). And then it is from the Father that he brings forth the Spirit upon the apostles. "After this he breathed on them and said 'Receive the Holy Spirit'" (Jn 20:22). Here, too, we see how the evangelist holds together in unity the Ascension, the giving of the Holy Spirit, and the Resurrection.

The early Church, spellbound by the mystery of God, saw the risen Christ as already exalted, transfigured and showering down heavenly gifts from his seat at God's right hand; and in the Paraclete, whom the Lord had promised and had sent on the fiftieth day, they did not see one who was in a sense separate from the Father and the Son, but who was the Spirit of Christ himself, the pneumatic Lord who is Spirit (2 Cor 3:17) and who therefore mediates the life of the Blessed Trinity to us. Even according to his humanity Christ became Spirit, and it is he who gives us the power and Spirit of God, which is no less than his life. The Holy Spirit comes to us through Christ with the Father and the Son, as John once again makes clear:

> I shall ask the Father, and he will give you another Advocate to be with you for ever, that Spirit of truth whom the world can

never receive since it neither sees nor knows him; but you know him, because he is with you, he is in you. I will not leave you orphans; I will come back to you. In a short time the world will no longer see me; but you will see me, because I live and you will live. On that day you will understand that I am in my Father and you in me and I in you. Anyone who receives my commandments and keeps them will be one who loves me; and anyone who loves me will be loved by my Father, and I shall love him and show myself to him... If anyone loves me he will keep my word, and my Father will love him, and we shall come to him and make our home with him. The Advocate, the Spirit, whom the Father will send in my name, will teach you everything and remind you of all I have said to you (Jn 14:16ff.).

In his own fashion, at once mystical and yet perfectly clear, St John explains that the Spirit is not separate from Christ, but is his gift, his Spirit. And the Fathers of the Church, too, stress that it is the *kyrios* who sends the Spirit, himself coming to us in the Spirit. But just as it is the Lord who sends the Spirit to us, conversely it is only in the Spirit that we recognize Jesus as the Son of God: "No one can say 'Jesus is Lord' unless he is under the influence of the Holy Spirit" (1 Cor 12:3).

Since the fourth century the Church has inclined more towards contemplation of the separate, historical aspects of the acts of God, but this did not cancel out the deeper, theological meaning of the feast of Easter. Pentecost, which blossomed out of the Pasch, is for all time the cult-mystery of redemption and exaltation. At Pentecost there is neither fasting nor kneeling. It is a time of uninterrupted exaltation and holy joy, a ceaseless Alleluia. Pentecost is the liturgical symbol of the perfection of the Church in the kingdom of Christ, of its coming to rest eternally in God. This will be complete when the whole number of the elect have fought their way through the Cross into the life of God. In a mystery, Pentecost is already the Sabbath promised to God's people; it is their transformation in eternal love, when the whole company of the redeemed, purified from sin and freed from all disquiet, will have become an offering to

God, and come to rest in the arms of God, singing the hymn of praise to the Blessed Trinity. All this is no mere glimpse into the future, no mere lightening of hope, but is already truth and fact. "Since you have been brought back to true life with Christ, you must look for the things that are in heaven, where Christ is, sitting at God's right hand. Let your thoughts be on heavenly things, not on the things that are on the earth, because you have died, and now the life you have is hidden with Christ in God" (Col 3:1-3). Ths applies to us now, and the next verse too will be fulfilled: "But when Christ is revealed—and he is your life—you too will be revealed in all your glory with him."

Pentecost means living by the present, divine power of Christ, which makes us capable of moral heroism. In the flesh our life is still Pasch, that is a transition, and it still stands under the sign of the Cross. We find ourselves in the gateway between the desert of the world and our home. The preview that Pentecost gives us of our home empowers us to follow the way of the Cross along with our Lord Jesus. But Pentecost also gives us the assurance that as Christians we are already living a new life that one day will issue victoriously into an eternally blessed Pentecost, and so come fully into its own.

9
The Ascension

The glorified Christ with Cross in hand

EARLY PICTURES OF Christ's ascension into heaven show him rising up to the Father, bearing the beam of the Cross upon his shoulder; or the Cross was depicted swinging beneath him, while he held his arms spread out wide in the form of a cross. Often there is no cross, but it is suggested by the Lord's prayerful attitude. In early Christian iconography the holy martyrs too—St Peter and St Lawrence, for example—like their Lord, the king of Martyrs, in their glory bear the cross. Thus Christ takes his Cross with him as he ascends in triumph to take possession of his throne of glory.

But there is more: in his glorious Second Coming, in the *parousia*, the day of his supreme outward triumph, Christ appears with the Cross. As the Lord ascended into heaven the angels said to the apostles, who were left behind: "...This Jesus, who has been taken up from you into heaven, will come in the same way as you saw him go into heaven" (Acts 1:11). The early Church, who had put the Cross in his hand, must therefore have expected to see the sign of the Cross at his Second Coming. *Hoc signum crucis erit in cælo, cum Dominus ad iudicandum venerit*—This sign of the Cross will be seen in heaven when the Lord comes in judgment.(1)

How ought we to interpret this? Certainly the Lord has risen above the Cross, leaving all earthly pain behind, all fear of death, all ignominy, and has exchanged these things for eternal glory. What place, then, has the Cross, sign of humiliation, bitter fruit of this earth, instrument of death, in the glory of heaven, in the bliss of the world to come, in the joy of divine everlasting life? But the Saviour carries it triumphantly to his throne on high, and his Church places the holy Cross upon her altars and sings praises to it. And the Church too, which has shared her Lord's victory, and has ascended with him to the Father, carries the Cross in her hand, as we see in the earliest iconography, which depicts the Church waving the banner of the Cross. As the Bridegroom glories in the Cross so does the Bride. *Nos autem gloriari oportet in cruce Domini nostri Iesu Christi*— We must glory in the Cross of our Lord Jesus.(2)

How can anyone glory in something that is the lowest and most ignominious thing there is? *Abi in crucem*—to the cross with you, was the nastiest insult a Roman could utter. The Jews put it this way: *Maledictus omnis qui pependit in ligno*—cursed is he who hangs upon the tree (Dt 21:23). How, then, can anyone glory in the Cross? To glory is to give expression to life in its fullest, to rejoice in an outburst of living energy. The Cross, on the other hand, is the suppression of all life and so of all joy; it is sadness, pain, and death. There is no life in this hard, cold stake, and whoever is nailed to it has the last breath and drop of blood squeezed out of him. And yet the Church says: in our crucified Lord Jesus Christ is our redemption, our life and our resurrection.

Through all of this we recognize that the Church truly is something heavenly. *Ecclesia in cælis*—the Church is in heaven. She comes down from heaven and from heaven she calls out to us: in the Cross there is redemption, life and resurrection! It is only when seen against the backdrop of heaven, only in the context of the depths of God and his totally other, inexhaustible wisdom, that such words make sense. From an earthly perspective they are sheer nonsense and folly.

It is heaven alone that can show us the true meaning of the mystery of the Cross; and that is why our Lord carries his Cross with him up to heaven.

The Cross is poised between heaven and earth. It is firmly rooted in the earth, but it towers right up into heaven. It binds heaven and earth together, and it separates heaven from earth. The fact that it binds them together is demonstrated especially by our Lord's first *parousia* in the flesh, when the Son of Man hung between heaven and earth on the Cross, and offered himself as a sacrifice for the human race who had become separated from heaven. That the Cross separates heaven and earth will be demonstrated by his second *parousia*, when the Cross will shine down from heaven upon earth, gathering the faithful together but pronouncing eternal judgment on the world.

At the first *parousia*, however, the Cross had united only in virtue of its power to separate. The Cross will always be the boundary between God and the world. God is able to step down into the world only if he crosses the boundary; and man can only rise up to God if he crosses over the boundary from his side. The "world" means the empire of sin, the world that is against God, the world that has risen up in rebellion and wants to know nothing about God. When God again offered salvation to this world, his only-begotten Son descended into the fearsome regions of sin and darkness and became like fallen man insofar as was consonant with his purity. He became as we sinners all are, but without sin. He assumed human flesh with all its horrors, misery, pain and death. That is to say he took up the Cross. By fastening upon the Cross the innocent body he had assumed from this world, he tore the world out of the grasp of sin. The Cross thus both separated and united: it separated insofar as it spoke emphatically of the fearful abyss that exists between God and the world—"the world murders God"—God dies because of sin; but it has united in that the victorious Crossbearer, in his body, leads redeemed mankind over into the kingdom of God. *Hodie mecum eris in paradiso*—today you will be with me in paradise, said the dying Lord to the penitent thief (Lk 23:43), and he says the same to all sinners who turn to him. The pharisees—and they represent the world that murders God—are forever separated from God by the Cross; the humble and contrite sinners, on the other hand, are forever reconciled and united with God by that same Cross. It is the same sign that brings death to the world and condemns it to eternal death, that brings life to the faithful. That life is not the earthly life of the flesh, not just human life, but holy, supernatural, divine life. Earthly life, all the exuberance and pride of the flesh has been submerged on the Cross; but there true and eternal life has risen. We can understand, therefore, why the Church glories in the Cross of life, and why she dates that life from the Resurrection: *in quo est vita et resurrectio nostra*—in him is our life and our resurrection. A new coming to life after the death of mortal life—that is the remarkable thing that the world cannot understand; at best it grudgingly accepts it. Earthly life ends in death, but the death of mortal life, if accepted for the sake of God, leads to eternal life. "If you sow to your own flesh, you will reap corruption from the flesh; but if you sow to the Spirit, you will reap eternal life from the Spirit" (Gal 6:8). This sowing in the Spirit requires the natural death of the seed-corn. "Unless a grain of wheat falls into the earth and dies, it remains just a single grain; but if it dies, it bears much fruit" (Jn 12:24).

Ever since our Lord died on the Cross, the Cross has increasingly shown itself to be the Tree of Life; it has become a heavenly mystery, a sacred symbol of life. The Lord had to bear its full weight upon himself. He knew that against him were ranged all the combined forces of sin, the whole strength of Satan. We can understand, therefore, why he trembled at the thought of the Cross, not so much from fear of pain and sacrifice as from disgust at the evil that lay before him and glared at him through the terrible eyes of hell. We all know how the soul is shaken to the core when faced with sin in its naked ugliness—through the devil's temptation, through our own guilt or through persecution by evil men. In such times our soul trembles and would fall to pieces but for the power of God supporting us. How grim it all must have appeared to Jesus on the Mount of Olives, when the sins of the whole world confronted him, threatening to engulf him. In spite of this our Lord went on to accept his passion, because he knew that this was his Father's will: *Fiat voluntas tua*—thy will be done (Mt 26:42).

Since then the Cross has become lighter for us. True, it still weighs down on our shoulders, but we know that there is another who carries it with us. *Dominus subponit suam*—the Lord upholds us with his hand (Ps 36:24), and he bears most of the weight. For all the burden, bearing it is a joy because the Lord is with us. *Noli timere, quia tecum ego sum, ut eruam te*—fear not, I am with you! I will raise you up (Jer 1:8). From the Lord's own Cross the strength comes to us to bear our crosses. *Tu es patientia mea, Domine*—you are my patience, O Lord! (Ps 70:5). It is not just our Lord's example that strengthens us, although it would be comfort, indeed, to have such a one as our precursor in carrying the Cross; it is that the grace and help we require actually flows to us from the Cross of the Lord. For us the Cross becomes a mystery, the effectual sign of divine power.

When our Lord left behind his Cross, the instrument of his death and token of his ignominy, and entered into heaven, paradoxically he took his Cross with him, but a Cross that now had a totally new significance. Or, better, he gave back to the Cross its true, eternal significance. Hitherto it had been misused by men as a tool of torment and insult and killing; now, in the hands of the Glorified its original meaning is restored. The Cross was originally a sign of all-embracing lordship and splendor. That is why ancient symbolism depicts the sun in the form of the swastika-cross—so often misused. The sun is the supreme glory of the visible world; its round disc with cruciform rays was seen in ancient times as the sign of its lordship over the natural world. The sun reigned over all four corners of the world and its power penetrated all things.

Understood in this sublime way, therefore, the cross was ideally suited to become an image of the true Sun-King, the *Sol iustitiae*—the Sun of Righteousness (Mal 3:20), who overcame the darkness of sin, and ascended up to his throne at God's right hand. And that same Cross is the sacred sign through which all divine power comes down to us.

For this reason the holy Cross is related to all of the mysteries of the Church. By it a person is signed at the very moment he enters the kingdom of God. We were born into the realm of purely natural life, that is into death. But the Church signs us with the sign of the Cross and thus confers upon us eternal life. We are baptized into the sacramental image of the Cross. And the mystical womb of Mother Church, the baptismal font, is itself signed with the Cross, so that it is able to give us birth into eternal life. When we go down into the font we go down into Christ's death, into his blood, we mount the Cross; and painlessly we are reborn. The Cross reveals itself to us as the *gloria crucis*, the bright glory of the Cross of which we boast, that it gives us superabundant, eternal life.

This life, however, is not yet assured us; it can be lost again as long as the death of sin threatens us. Nor does it yet dwell in us in its fullness, but only in its beginnings, as a pledge. That which we have gained from the mystery must be repossessed daily; it must be confirmed and defended against attacks, must be increased. In this task it is once again the Cross that is our most effective tool, not in the glory of the mystery, but in its sober, unprepossessing, everyday dress. Here it is a case of following our Lord with his Cross on his earthly paths, which are sprinkled with his blood. We walk with relentless effort along the wearisome and often monotonous path of *conversatio morum*, of moral conversion, never laying down the tool of the Cross—day or night. This way of the Cross will seem to lead with ever diminishing comfort deeper and deeper down into darkness, where all earthly light fails; but above hangs the glory of the Cross, the sacred mystery. Invisibly this strengthens us, so that we do not lose heart, but move on unerringly towards our eternal goal. Step by step, almost imperceptibly, the grey, everyday Cross changes into the radiant Cross of eternity. Even while still on earth we can catch glimpses of this glory, as when one senses a greater freedom in God, when one's spirit rejoices in the Saviour. But a time is coming when the glory of the Cross will be fully revealed. When all earthly strength and beauty ebb from us and our bodies seem to be extinguished, and we hang on the Cross like our naked, agonized Lord, then we are only a hair's breadth away from the glory of the Cross, just as on Good Friday our Lord was only a hair's breadth away from the glory of the Resurrection. Blessed will we then be if our whole life long we have patiently and laboriously carried our cross of pain behind our Lord. Then he will transform it into a Cross of glory that we can take up with us into the eternal triumph of heaven.

10
Pentecost

The Spirit—God gives himself to mankind

On Pentecost the fifty days of the feast have come to an end—or rather, they have reached their peak and fulfillment. The whole festival—so immensely full of content—comes to an end on the feast of Pentecost. The total wealth of the feast has been displayed before our eyes and bequeathed to us as the ripe fruit of the Spirit. With the apostles we have been sent out into the whole world—each in his own way—as ambassadors of the power of the Spirit. "And he said to them, 'Go out to the whole world; proclaim the Good News to all creation'" (Mk 16:15). And to what must we bear witness? "He who believes and is baptized will be saved" (Mk 16:16). Through faith and baptism we gain salvation—eternal life. And so the Spirit spreads knowledge of the Pasch throughout the whole world, for faith and baptism are gifts of the Pasch, gifts of the Cross, gifts of the Resurrection; for only those who, with the Lord, die to the world and rise for God can enter, through faith, into the heavenly kingdom. And baptism is the mystery of this dying and rising.

The feast celebrated at Pentecost once again sums up the whole content of the Pasch. But what *is* the Pasch? It is God's revelation to the human race. What is revelation? As the scriptures put it, revelation is the "unveiling" of the divine mystery, and hence its communication to mankind. God has lifted the veil that conceals his essence. Through Christ he has allowed us to glimpse his mystery. We were blind and deaf and dumb; we were people who walked in the sunlight but never saw the sun; we were sunk in the deep abyss of sin and ignorance. God's infinite life was flowing past us and we were quite unaware of it; indeed we regarded our own light—that was no better than darkness—as better and brighter than the sun that is God. We knew nothing of God's inexhaustible love. The fires of eternity were burning while we sat in the cold. We knew nothing of the truth but sat in the shadow of death and error. We had no conception of God's beauty, in which alone we can find blessedness, but allowed ourselves to be distraught by the horrid evidence of our abandonment, or else tried to comfort ourselves with the deceitful pleasures of the world, which stink of corruption and dead men's bones.

Then the almighty and merciful God took pity on us and lifted the veil. "No one has ever seen God; it is the only Son, who is nearest to the Father's heart, who has made him known" (Jn 1:18). From all eternity he looked upon the Father; he is the fruit of the Father's love and eternal generation; he is able to speak to us about what he has seen. But he could not pass this on to us all at once, for our eyes were incapable of looking upon God. It would have killed us were we to have gazed suddenly into the rays of the sun. And so he had to heal us, to open our eyes and to strengthen them, so that they acquired the faculty of looking upon the mystery. That was why he had first to mount the Cross in order, through his unspeakable agony, to bring us salvation, to cure us of sin's sickness. He took all of our infirmities upon himself and destroyed them in himself upon the Cross. Having taken away our mortal illness there upon the Cross, he was able to raise the curtain that kept the kingdom of God hidden from our eyes. Until then even the light of God that shone in him had been veiled for us; but now his humanity became a luminous, transparent curtain through which we could see the light of God, without becoming blinded. "By your light we see the light" (Ps 36:10). "In other words, brothers, through the blood of Jesus we have the right to enter the sanctuary by a new way which he has opened for us, a living opening through the curtain, that is to say, his body. And we have the supreme high priest over all the house of God. So as we go in, let us be sincere in heart and filled with faith..." (Heb 11:19ff.). The Lord, now risen in the power of the Spirit, completely transfigured and received in his sacred humanity by God the Father, is our mystagogue, who leads us into the holy of holies and gives us eternal life.

> And eternal life is this: to know you, the one true God, and Jesus Christ whom you have sent (Jn 17:3).

Who gives us this knowledge? The Holy Spirit. First of all he allows us to recognize the Father's emissary, the God-man, in his true nature, that is as Spirit and God. "No one can say 'Jesus is Lord' unless he is under the influence of the Holy Spirit" (1 Cor 12:3). Like knows like. For this reason we must first—in our own style—become like the Lord in order truly to recognize him. Jesus became Lord through the Cross, having become obedient even to the extent of accepting the Cross. We too have to cast off the old, earthly man through taking up our crosses; we have to become conformed to Christ's death through baptism and by our daily carrying of our crosses, so that we become like him in his exaltation to the Father's side. Then we will receive in ourselves the life of Christ, the Holy Spirit, and through the Spirit, become capable of recognizing Christ as he really is: the only-begotten Son of God, the Lord who is the Father's equal in divinity and who has been taken up, in his humanity, into the life of the Blessed Trinity. Recognizing him, thus we have become like him, for like recognizes like. We become sons and daughters of God, sharing in the glory of him who is full of grace and truth. All of this is given us by the Holy Spirit, who is Christ's life. "Now this Lord is the Spirit,..." (2 Cor 3:17). He promised to send another Paraclete, but it is he who comes to us in this Paraclete. He said: "I will not leave you orphans; I will come back to you" (Jn 14:18). And he continues: "It is for your own good that I am going because unless I go, the Advocate will not come to you" (Jn 16:7). How can we reconcile: "I am going away" with "and shall return" (Jn 14:28)? The one who goes is the one who returns. He returns in his heavenly being as the exalted one, to give them a share in the life of God. As the Fathers of the Church say, he takes away from them the *praesentia corporalis*, the physical appearance, and gives back to them the *praesentia spiritualis*, the spiritual presence. His humanity has now become a transparent curtain through which we see the Godhead himself. "Through Christ the man to Christ who is God" (Augustine). In this way, through the Spirit, we recognize our Lord Jesus Christ as the Son of God, as equal to the Father, and hence our way to the Father. "In a short time the world will no longer see me; but you will see me, because I live and you will live. On that day you will understand that I am in my Father and you in me and I in you" (Jn 14:19f.). "Anybody who loves me will be loved by my Father, and I shall love him and show myself to him" (Jn 14:21).

Had Christ not been the true Son of God, consubstantial with the Father, we could not have reached the Father through him. We would have remained far from God. Only the true Son can lead us to the true Father, "And eternal life is this: *to know you the only true God*" (Jn 17:3). *God* has *revealed* himself through *Jesus Christ*. The New Covenant is the revelation of the *Blessed Trinity*. The Trinity is the interior life of the Godhead. If then, in Christ, God unveils his trinitarian life to us, he is permitting us to share in the mystery of the eternal Godhead at the very deepest level. Between human beings the highest degree of love is shown when one allows the other to share in his interior life. Therein is supreme trust, perfect communication, total self-giving. Love is nothing other than sharing life together, with all that we possess, at the deepest level. What love, what a gift, what a vocation, to be permitted to see into the inner life of God! Under the Old Covenant God revealed himself as *Lord*; under the New Covenant he has revealed himself as *Father*, who in his eternal love forever generates the Son in his heart, giving himself completely to him; but both Father and Son are one in the breath that is the Holy Spirit. By revelation we see into the Father's heart, where Father and Son meet in the Spirit's eternal embrace. One Being in three Persons! Here is the most personal love, the most personal generation and breathing forth, and yet only *one* Being. We cannot do more than stammer about this mystery of divine being and life. But as we read holy scripture we sense something of this limitless plenitude of life, of love, and of knowledge.

By revealing this mystery to us, God has made us a gift of himself, has bared his innermost self to us. Not only has he *shown* himself to us; he has also *shared* himself with us, so that we are drawn into his innermost life. The mystery is no mere theatrical show: it demands audience participation. Looking upon God, we become divinized, become swept away in a flood of intra-divine life. "We shall come to him and make our home with him" (Jn 14:23). God becomes our guest because we are his guests. The unity of the Blessed Trinity becomes our unity, for the Lord prayed: "I have given them the glory you gave to me, that they may be one as we are one. With me in them and you in me, may they be so completely one that the world will realize that it was you who sent me...I have made your name known to them and will continue to make it known, so that the love with which you loved me may be in them, and so that I may be in them" (Jn 17:22ff.).

All of this is a gift of the Holy Spirit, sent us by Christ. That for which he prayed, Christ gave to his disciples and to all of us after his exaltation, when he breathed on them and said: "Receive the Holy Spirit" (Jn 20:22). Today, on the feast of Pentecost, he has bestowed this Spirit of *agape* and unity upon the whole Church. Within the Trinity, Father and Son always act in the Spirit, and through the Spirit, who indeed proceeds from the Father and the Son. The Holy Spirit, who is the third Person and perfects the Trinity, is the Person who acts outwardly towards the creation. But the Spirit does not act on its own, but in union with the Father and the Son. The third Person is the Father's gift to the Son and the Son's gift to the Father; for the Spirit flows from Father to Son and the Son gives back this life to the Father. That is why the third Person is called the Spirit. If the Holy Spirit—the giving within the Trinity—were not consubstantial with the Father and the Son, that gift would be less than God. The Spirit is thus *the* Holy Spirit, "who with the Father and the Son is worshipped and glorified" (Creed).

The same may be said about the Spirit as the Trinity's gift to us. The Spirit is Christ's great Easter gift, a gift from the Father and the Son—"the promise of the Father" (Acts 1:4, cf. 2:33). It is the Messianic gift promised to the kingdom of God. Pentecost is the celebration of the gift of the Holy Spirit. It is not as if at Pentecost, having celebrated the first and second Persons, we now celebrate the third on its own. No, in the Spirit God reveals himself as the great gift of heaven to mankind. And so, for us the Spirit is first and foremost *the* Spirit, *the* gift. What an immense honor, that the Holy Spirit should be poured out on all flesh! It is true that God would seem to demean himself by climbing down into our humble dwelling. And yet it is no demeaning of God but rather an exaltation of the Creator through the glorifying of his creation. Just as Jesus was glorified through his passion and resurrection, so the Holy Spirit is glorified as it reveals his *agape*, for this gift is the divine *agape* itself.

Does the Holy Spirit lose something of its divine dignity, its honor as a Person by becoming a gift? By no means! The Spirit that is poured out upon all flesh, that comes to dwell in the Church and in the individual soul is at once a divine Person and one with the Father and the Son. Were it *merely* a gift it would have to be less than the Father and the Son; and then it would not be the gift of *God*, but of something created. It follows that once again we would be neither in nor with God. But if the Spirit is more than mere gift, and is in fact the Giver as well, not just the Father's tool but itself the source of all graces, then through the Holy Spirit we are in truth with God himself. This is therefore the new Paraclete alongside Jesus Christ. Nor is it just alongside, but is *with* him and *in* him. The Spirit is, for sure, in its divine essence, one with the *logos*, which is the Personhood of the God-man.

The Holy Sprit is our nearest and dearest relative; it is *with* us and remains *in* us. It is the innermost life of our soul, although it is forever high above us, as God is high and exalted over all created beings. The same Being who dwells in my soul, and constitutes my innermost life, sits enthroned with the Father and the Son. The Person who seals the bond between Father and Son is the Person who unites me with the Father and the Son; and our blessedness and our glory derive from both of these bonds. Were the Spirit not one with the Father and with the Son we would not be with God; were the Spirit not to live in us we would not be in God. Through the Spirit that is imparted to us we enter into the eternity of God, and remain forever as creatures of *agape*, subject to the Lord in the everlasting *agape* that is himself.

Through grace we carry this heavenly guest in our hearts. St Paul admonished the Ephesians to do good, "otherwise you will only be grieving the Holy Spirit of God who has marked you with his seal" (Eph 4:30). Live by the Holy Spirit; act through the Holy Spirit; pray in the same Spirit; do not quench the Spirit, but fan it into life or, rather, let it fan you into life—enkindle you and inspire you. In these days how could we possibly live as Christians apart from the Spirit. Look at the apostles! See how they were transformed by the Spirit! At first they had doubted, still seeking an earthly kingdom, full of fear and dread. All at once all fear was blown away in the blast of the heavenly gale. The Spirit conquers the world, liberates the world, judges the world. It gives us superhuman strength. The Spirit *is* Christ's victory over the world; it is the power of God. Today it still possesses the power to renew both us and the whole world, and bear us up to God.

"Send forth your Spirit, O Lord, and renew the face of the earth" (Ps 103:30).

11
The Assumption of Mary into heaven

Abandonment to God is the way to life

On this feast day we celebrate the Dormition of the Blessed Virgin Mary—in other words, the memorial of her death. Some may be horrified to hear the word "death" in this context, for the festival is totally suffused with an atmosphere of peace and beauty. We are scarcely aware of the fact of death. For us it is the first, beautiful day of spring.

On other saints' feast days it is the same. Death has been swallowed up in victory. On 10 August, a few days before the Assumption, we celebrate the feast of the deacon Lawrence. What a terrible death! We see the grid-iron, the mangled, blood-spattered, smoking body of this holy man. Even in all of this, triumph predominates. Pope St Leo the Great addressed Lawrence's persecutors thus:

> You accomplish nothing by this horrific act of violence. All substance is removed from your designs, and because Lawrence has gone to heaven, you become as nothing. Your

flames could never quench the flame of the *agape* of Christ. The fire that burns before our eyes is weaker than the fire that glows inwardly. Your fury, O tormentors, have served the martyr well. You have augmented his merit by piling on the torment. Everything that your ingenuity has devised has worked only for the glory of God, and even the instruments of torture have become the sign of triumph.

If we are filled with joy and thanksgiving as we look upon the gruesome death of this martyr, seeing behind the outward horror the undying glory of God, how much more easily can we see beyond the sting of death, and experience the joy and glory of triumph when we meditate on the peaceful falling asleep of the Blessed Virgin Mary? What is the fundamental meaning of this event?

It is a primeval human concept, or rather a divine concept that has been revealed to man, that no good thing can come about *except through* sacrifice. Man's supreme sacrifice, however, is himself, and he makes this sacrifice when he yields up his whole life. The simplest and most primitive expression of such sacrifice is the giving up of life in death. In this way a man gives all that he can possibly give. "What has a man to offer in exchange for his life?" (Mt 16:26), says our Lord. In primeval times, before mankind had been corrupted by culture, men and women—as we know—gave up themselves or the things they valued most, in death. We know how a king, having ruled his people for, say, ten years, would publicly sacrifice himself, so as to hand on the power of life to his people. We know how a general would hurl himself into the enemy lines, so as to ensure victory for his army. We know how a nobleman would sacrifice his only son, so as to protect his land from attack by a mighty aggressor. We know of nations that were prepared to throw their finest young men and most beautiful girls to a monster in order to have their fatherland spared. We know of builders of cities who buried their children in the foundations so as to guarantee perpetual safety for that city. Everywhere there is evidence of sacrifice, the sacrifice of life. Moreover, this sacrifice was not celebrated in mourning and lament, but with joy that issued out from the deepest pain and ended in triumph; for the object of the sacrifice was to preserve, protect, and enhance life. It was an attempt to make life everlasting. Without sacrifice there is no life. Sacrifice per se, that is the person sacrificed gives himself up gladly, because he knows that he is bringing life to his people and that therefore he is being raised up onto a divine plane: he is entering into the eternal life of the deity. "I have willingly given all this" (1 Chron 29:17). Death is the source of life; the point of death is the gateway into a higher life. "No, I shall not die, I shall live" (Ps 117:17). For this reason sacrifices were adorned and draped with costly materials; they were made to look like brides going to meet their bridegrooms. "I bring holocausts to your house, I bring them to fulfill those vows that rose to my lips..." (Ps 66:13).

What is it that we ought to see behind these apparently horrific customs of ancient times? There is no doubt that we detect the feeling that no one can reach the world of the gods except through giving up this mortal life, and that the higher life has to be nourished by abandonment of the life of the flesh. "Tell it only to the wise, whom the common crowd despise, that I commend only that life which longs to be consumed in fire" (Goethe). These customs are a faint sensing of the truth that the eternal life of God can become our portion only after all that is earthly about us has been sacrificed. Anyone who clings doggedly to what is of earth can never share in the divine. In harmony with these thoughts is the leap into the uncertain abyss, the descent into the depths of death. The ancients knew a kind of death wish. The purple deep, symbolized and reached by blood, was an object of trembling love. Plato said that the whole life of a philosopher was only a rehearsal for death.

Here we meet sacrifice through death at a higher level. Primitive men offered life, blood. Every sacrifice required the shedding of blood: "If there is no shedding of blood there is no remission" (Heb 9:22). Forgiveness of sins along with the enhancement of life is the goal and meaning of sacrifice. In the last analysis, however, it is only a removal of the barrier between God and man. Sin is death, and if by the death of the flesh sin is removed in the sacrifice, the way to life is left open. The concept of sin has thus refined the concept of sacrifice. Gradually men and women came to see that they had to be liberated not just externally and ritually from sin, but had to turn their backs on sin through inward repentance. In this way sacrifice became sublimated. No longer was the bloody killing, but the dying of the interior man the essence of sacrifice. We find a clear statement of this in Psalm 51, wherein the sinful king confesses his guilt and is prepared to offer sacrifice: "Sacrifice gives you no pleasure, were I to offer holocaust you would not have it. My sacrifice is a broken spirit, you will not scorn this crushed and broken heart" (Ps 51:16f.). In this sacrifice it is the inner man, the real man, who dies. This is no mere fleshly offering but a spiritual one. It is hard to give up one's bodily life, but it is much harder to give up one's inner self, to die the *mystical* death; but we cannot realize within ourselves the divine life unless our self-will is first destroyed. Bodily death makes sense only if it symbolizes this *mystical* death. This mystical death can, however, occur quite independently.

In our Lord we see both forms of sacrifice united. He died, a bloody sacrifice on the Cross. That was a wholly primitive form of sacrifice. The Father himself offered up his beloved, only-begotten Son, punishing the sin which out of love the Son had taken upon himself, and forming out of the Son's life the life of the world.

In doing this God had carried out that primitive form of sacrifice which he had required of Abraham, but then canceled. The Son gave himself up to death in order to destroy sinful flesh and, through the shedding of his blood, to give life to the whole world. In this act his blood was made the cup of salvation, the blood of the new and eternal covenant with God. The Son offered himself "through eternal Spirit" (Heb 9:14), that is his sacrifice was the total yielding up of his Spirit to the Father's will. Thus Christ's death is the most comprehensive form of sacrifice. In the history of Christianity the two forms of sacrifice again become separated. Lawrence the martyr represents the blood-sacrifice. In his case his bodily frame was violently mangled and destroyed in order to demonstrate to the world that everything that desires to come to God must forfeit its earthly existence. The martyr bears witness to the world's sinfulness, its attachment to the flesh. He himself is freed from sin through his blood: "They have washed their robes in the blood of the Lamb" (Apoc 7:14), that is to say, the martyr's blood flows into the blood of our sacrificed Lord, and so becomes the cup of life. Baptism of blood, first endured by the Lord, is also experienced by the martyr. He receives the cup of blood from the hand of his King, and drinks it: for him it becomes the "cup of eternal salvation."

Representatives of the *spiritual sacrifice* by itself are the Blessed Virgin Mary, St John the Evangelist, and many other confessors and virgins. In them we see not so much the atonement through blood and a violent severing of ties with this earthly life as a calm, gentle, consecrated transition into the kingdom of God. "If I want him to stay behind till I come, what does it matter to you?" (Jn 21:23) the Lord said to Peter concerning John. This did not mean that John would never die, but that he would enter non-violently into the kingdom of God. "There are some of those standing here who will not taste death before they see the Son of Man coming with his kingdom" (Mt 18:28). Mary too grew into the kingdom of her Son in quietness and peace. That does not mean that she was not to die. As a daughter of Eve, she too had to pay the price. But for her, bodily death was only a transition into that life which she had already been enjoying for a long time. *Mystically* she died with her Son as she stood beneath the Cross. Indeed it was earlier—when she said: "Let what you have said be done to me" (Lk 1:18). And so, for her, bodily death had lost all of its horror; there was no longer any violence or fear about it. "O death, where is your sting?" (1 Cor 15:55) is specially appropriate in respect to Mary. For the Christian, death speaks not of annihilation, but of passing over into the fullness of life. Whoever has experienced mystical death does not in a sense need to die bodily. Bodily death is then only the seal put upon what has long been a reality. It is a casting off of the last obstacle that still defers entry into the fullness of life.

That is why the death of the Blessed Virgin Mary is celebrated with quiet, peaceful triumph. She was a perfect sacrifice, utterly consumed in the fire of *agape*, transfigured by her vision of God, and totally consecrated to God by the Spirit. She had no need of any violent blood-shedding, but only of her final *assumption* into heaven. "Mary has been assumed into heaven amid the rejoicing of the angels" (Gradual of the Mass).

It is noteworthy, that the virgin-martyrs were venerated primarily as virgins. This may well indicate that virginity was seen as so great a spiritual sacrifice that it eclipsed martyrdom. Properly understood, virginity is a spiritual sacrifice. Virgins who renounce marriage, not because they want to avoid the sacrifices that marriage demands, nor out of a lack of natural affection, but solely because they want to offer themselves in complete detachment from the world so as to be totally consecrated to God, are themselves a spiritual sacrifice. They are already dead to this world. "I have been crucified with Christ" (Gal 2:19). Their earthly existence is already extinguished, and they are already sons and daughters of the resurrection. For this reason the virgin-martyrs' bloody deaths are not stressed so much, not because they did not have to die, but because they were already mystically dead.

Mary is *virgo virginum*, virgin of virgins; her motherhood did not diminish, but consecrated her virginity. Genuine virginity is thus not physical virginity but spiritual oblation to God, total offering of the self to the divine life.

Sacrifice is joy—we learn that this is so from the feast of the Assumption of the Blessed Virgin Mary. Had it not been for her absolute surrender to the will of God, her pain and the sword that pierced her soul as she stood at the foot of the Cross, had it not been for her perfect union with her glorified Son, Mary would not have been caught up into the heavenly bliss which we celebrate on this festival. We too, if we offer ourselves body and soul, and accept death according to the will of God in whatever form it comes to us, will experience life blossoming out of death. The annihilation of our earthly existence will become the birth of our new humanity.

"For you, O Lord, are the glory of their strength; by your favor it is that our might is exalted" (Ps 89:19). "Blessed is he whom you choose and call to dwell in your courts. We are filled with the blessings of your house, of your holy temple" (Ps 65:5).

12
Peter and Paul

The meaning of devotion to the saints

THE LITURGICAL CULT of the saints, that is the cult as practiced in the Church, is distinguished from popular devotion, in that it regards the saints not as isolated individuals who to some extent live close to God, each with his own area of influence, but as *members in the Body of Christ*. In the saints it is Christ who is venerated, and in Christ, God. Therefore on saints' feast days we sing: *Regem apostolorum Dominum, Regem martyrum Dominum, Regem virginum Dominum.* That is, "Let us worship the King, the King of apostles, of martyrs, of virgins." And we sing also: *Regem regum Dominum, venite adoremus, quia ipse est coronum sanctorum omnium.* That is "Let us worship the Lord, the King of kings, he is the crown of all the saints." All of the saints are kings, they are "a line of kings, priests to serve" (Apoc 1:6 & 5:10); but they are all subjects of Christ the King. He is their royal diadem, their crown and garland; apart from him they are nothing. Through him they have become holy, for " only one is holy, only one is Lord, only one is the Most High–Jesus Christ."

Jesus Christ, however, is King of all saints in a very special sense. It is from his holiness that all holiness flows, for only one is holy—God. In the Old Testament Hannah sings: "There is none as holy as the Lord, indeed, there is no one but you" (1 Sam 2:2). But divine holiness flows into us through the man Jesus. This man is like us, "the eldest of many brothers" (Rom 8:29). Thus he also ranks first among many saints; for his human nature is not holy *in itself*, but is sanctified by the indwelling holiness of God, first through the hypostatic union and then through his glorification after his passion, of which the Lord himself says, "for their sake I consecrate myself so that they too may be consecrated in truth" (Jn 17:19). And even though our Lord, after his incarnation, was called by Peter "the holy one of God" (Jn 6:19), of his own free will he allowed himself to appear in sinful flesh. When, after the crucifixion, this had been destroyed, he was revealed as the perfectly Holy One who was numbered as the first-born amongst those who were to be sanctified. In his humanity also, therefore, he is the first, is the King of all saints. His holiness too flows entirely from God.

> It was appropriate that God, for whom everything exists and through whom everything exists, should make perfect, through suffering, the leader who would take them to their salvation. For the one who sanctifies and those who are sanctified, are of the same stock; that is why he openly calls them brothers (Heb 2:10ff.).

Our Lord's holiness flows from God the Father; nonetheless it is not a derived holiness. The Lord was perfected in his passion; he won his holiness. In his holiness grace and free cooperation worked together. The uncreated holiness of the *Logos* joined with the created holiness of the man Jesus, which again proceeded totally from the former holiness. As King of all saints our Lord demonstrates to us the mysterious cooperation between divine, sanctifying power and human self-sanctification. These cannot be separated. The saints all fashioned themselves on Christ's model, although not in the same measure.

In the saints, therefore, we venerate the God-man, Jesus Christ, the Son of God, our Lord. He, the Mediator between God and man, is the source of all holiness because he is God who is the giver of all holiness; and God bestows holiness only through his beloved Son. All human holiness is God's gift, is God's Spirit, the divine seed in mankind. Thus, in Christ, God has created saints for himself out of his own unity as a unity in the Spirit. "From all peoples" he has formed a chosen company, his *ecclesia*. It is because of this unity, and because it is born of grace and the gift of the Holy Spirit, that it is called the one, holy Bride, the *Una Sancta Ecclesia*.

And so, in the saints we venerate the Church; and in the Church we venerate her Lord and Bridegroom—Christ himself. Christ and the Church together are "the Christ" as St Paul declares in 1 Cor 12:12. For his part, Christ is there for the Father, and when all of the saints have been gathered together into the Body of Christ the Son will hand over his kingdom to the Father, so that God will be all in all (1 Cor 15:28). All holiness thus flows back into its source in the eternal Father-God, fulfilling the Lord's words: "I came from the Father and have come into the world and now I leave the world to go to the Father" (Jn 16:28).

Some people say that the saints come between us and God and Christ. That is not so. When properly venerated they introduce us to the *ecclesia*, to Christ and to the Father, for they are images of Christ, illuminated by his radiance. Clement of Alexandria wrote of Christians, that is of the saints:

> We are the people who, like living, walking statues, carry about with us in our humanity an image that dwells in us, reasons within us, is very intimate with us, suffers with us and yet is in control of the passions; for Christ we are a votive

icon to God, 'a chosen race, a royal priesthood, a consecrated nation, a people set apart...once not a people but now the People of God'; we are those of whom St John said, that they are not from below, but are those who have learned all things from him who came down from above, those who have recognized God's plan of salvation; we are those who know well how 'to walk in newness of life.'(1)

To cultivate fellowship with the saints is therefore to cultivate fellowship with Christ.

Not all saints, however, are alike; there is great variety within the Church. "The daughter of the king is clothed with splendor" (Ps 45:14). The divine archetype is so immense and all-embracing that it can never be reflected in one person. The charismata are distributed, therefore, amongst the saints. There are saints who reflect Christ in glory with a special immediacy and in whom we see Christ himself without, as it were, any intervening member.

Among such saints we count first and foremost the apostles. They appear to us like Christ himself. As Christ is the apostle of the Father, so they are apostles of Christ. "As the Father sent me so am I sending you" (Jn 20:21). Christ stands before us in the apostles. We could say that in Christ we see realized the tragedy of every apostolic person. It is well-known that those whom God sends are as a rule misunderstood, attacked and persecuted. This too was our Lord's fate, as he so often predicted it would be. But he knew that after his sacrifice on the Cross, others would gather in the harvest. John records his saying: "Here the proverb holds good: one sows, another reaps; I sent you to reap a harvest you had not worked for. Others worked for it; and you have come into the rewards of their trouble" (Jn 4:37f.).

After our Lord's departure from human sight and his return to the Father's right hand, the apostles came onto the scene in his place. They were his visible extension, so to speak. In the steps of the apostles our Lord's feet walked the whole world.

"Anyone who listens to you listens to me" (Lk 10:16). The Preface for the feast of the apostles runs: "Through the apostles you watch over and protect us always. You made them shepherds of the flock to share in the work of your Son...." In this way the *pastor aeternus*, the Eternal Shepherd, has not abandoned his flock, but pastures them still from heaven, unseen but with great power. Besides this he has given his flock visible representatives of his pastoral care.

The apostles possess the Lord's Spirit in special fullness. He gave them this immediately on rising from the dead. He breathed on them and imparted himself totally to them, gave them all of his power and his *agape*. "Simon, son of Jona, do you love me?...Then feed my sheep" (Jn 21:17). The Lord himself speaks to us through the apostles.

The Church received its shape from the apostles; Christ formed the Church through the apostles. On account of this it became known as "apostolic." From then on it was *una sancta apostolica*, the one, holy, apostolic Church. Because the apostles are *Christ living on*, and because the Church, as the Bride of Christ, is wholly constituted by his essence, apostolicity is of the essence of the Church. All that is apostolic is essential to the Church; anything that is not apostolic is non-essential or even a falsification. Apostolicity is the hallmark of the Church, of true doctrine, of genuine worship, and of pure love.

> So you are no longer aliens or foreign visitors; you are citizens like all the saints, and part of God's household. You are part of a building that has the apostles and prophets for its foundation, and Christ Jesus himself for its main cornerstone. As every structure is aligned on him, all grow into one holy temple in the Lord; and you too, in him, are being built into a house where God lives in the Spirit (Eph 2:9-22).

Christ is the cornerstone that supports and holds together the whole Church; none can take over from him this function. He is also the foundation and "nobody can lay any other than the one which has already been laid, that is Jesus Christ" (1 Cor 3:11). In the function of foundation, however, the Lord lets himself be represented by the apostles who possess his Spirit.

In a special way Peter and Paul are foundations of the Church. In them the Lord has built mighty and firm foundation walls for the whole edifice of the Church, sinking them deep down into the earthly substance of mankind. Each bears the weight of the Church in his own particular way.

Peter, the Rock, bears the Church up by his *authority*, by the power of binding and loosing, by ruling, commanding and judging. We have to distinguish Peter the man from Peter's office. In personality he was the good-natured, simple, affectionate disciple of Jesus, a fatherly teacher of the faithful. But in terms of his office he was the Rock, the judge. In this function he lives on in the Church, the symbol of hierarchy and hence of authority.

True Church authority is apostolic and hence Christ-like, that is, divine.

There is only one genuine authority—God. God is the Creator to whom all things belong and whom all must obey. God is the eternal truth from whom all other truth derives. God is eternal justice; what he orders is fair and right. God is the sole power with whom all must come to terms. God is the eternal law to which all things must conform. God is eternal *agape*, and it is in this that in the end all authority resides because eternal, selfless *agape* has no favorites: it is God-like.

The one and only authority that is visible is Christ. He is truly "the Word of the Father," the emissary of the Father, his apostle. It is he who gives us the new and eternal law. "The Lord gives the law" (2). Peter asked: "Lord, who shall we go to? You have the message of eternal life, and we believe; we know that you are the Holy One of God" (Jn 6:68f.). Christ is the loving will of the Father made flesh, and so we abandon ourselves to him without reservation. "You are the Christ, the Son of the living God" said Peter (Mt 16:17).

Through Christ, the apostles are the one and only true authority. All genuine authority in the Church flows from Christ through the apostles. As a rule Catholics let themselves be carried along on this authority; they swim, half asleep, in a stream of God's loving will. Only when temptation comes, when something threatens to give way, when their lodestar is dimmed, do they become aware of what apostolic authority means to them.

Those whom God has called to be leaders in the Church must, by faith, know that their authority rests solely upon Christ. Peter wrote:

> Now I have something to tell you elders: I am an elder myself, and a witness of the sufferings of Christ, and with you I have a share in the glory that is to be revealed. Be shepherds of the flock of God that is entrusted to you: watch over it, not simply as a duty but gladly, because God wants it; not for sordid money, but because you are eager to do it. Never be a dictator over any group that is put in your charge, but be an example that the whole flock can follow (1 Pet 5:1ff.).

Faith and love protect the representative of apostolic authority from all worldly desire for power and self-interest. Only in the Spirit may he teach about the things of the Spirit and of God, without introducing any earthly additives to the wheat of God.

Anyone who takes his stand upon apostolic authority takes his stand upon God. Not for nothing was Peter called the Rock. Through holy, divine, apostolic authority we are firmly set upon the rock that is God, and are ourselves made into people of rock, against whom the gates of hell can never prevail, provided that we persevere in pure, supernatural faith and self-less *agape*, solidly embedded within the *una sancta apostolica*.

Paul too was a hierarch, a leader and judge of the faithful. He, however, bore up the Church in rather a different manner;

and this is what makes Paul—as we still see him—a symbol of our fundamental concept of the Church. In Paul's case we do not have to make such a sharp distinction between the man and the office. First and foremost he portrays the pneumatic foundation of the Church, whereas Peter had portrayed the foundation. If one views the essence of the Church correctly this foundation is even more important than the other. Law vanishes with this aeon, but the Spirit remains forever. What Paul said with pride, but with true humility is relevant here: "By God's grace that is what I am, and the grace that he gave me has not been fruitless. On the contrary, I, or rather the grace of God that is with me, have worked harder than any of the others" (1 Cor 15:10).

"The grace of God with me"—these words of Paul point to the ultimate spiritual foundation of the Church: it is God's grace, God's Spirit that creates the Church, holds it together, bears it up.

Let us examine more closely the extent to which Paul takes up a special position in respect of this foundation.

First, Paul's *whole being* was built upon grace. "Through grace I am what I am." Grace had taken up his nature and transformed it, had tailored it afresh and transfigured it.

Paul was a Pharisee. Pharisees were men of great moral energy, of fervent zeal for God's will as revealed in the Law. Their view of God was voluntaristic, that is God in their eyes was Lord and law-giver, whose will had to be obeyed down to the last detail. And because God's law seemed to them to have too wide a mesh, they supplemented it with their own traditions, adding paragraph upon paragraph down to the smallest detail. Paul outstripped all of them in his fanatical zeal for the Law. "I stood out among the Jews of my generation, and how enthusiastic I was for the traditions of my ancestors" (Gal 1:14). This explains why he hated Jesus and his followers so much. He saw how this new way led away from the Law into totally wider fields. He regarded this as dangerous laxity, and as a dissolution of the

Law. When Stephen was executed for having spoken against the Temple and for proclaiming the passing away of Judaism, Saul was there keeping an eye on the clothes of the executioners. Stephen's remark: "You stubborn people, with your pagan hearts and pagan ears. You are always resisting the Holy Spirit, just as your ancestors used to. Can you name a single prophet your ancestors never persecuted?" (Acts 7:51ff.). He believed, as Jesus had predicted, that he would be glorifying God by destroying Jesus' disciples, just as they were intent on destroying the Law.

And then this same Jesus, who had appeared to Stephen as he died, hovered over Paul and struck him, the Pharisee, to the ground. It was a new man who rose up, a chosen vessel, a creation of grace. The Lord wanted to show him how much he would have to suffer for the sake of his name (Acts 9:15). Suffering means giving oneself up to the Cross and therefore to grace. The fanaticism of the Pharisee, proud of his own virtue, had been broken. He described himself as the "least of the apostles; in fact, since I persecuted the Church of God, I hardly deserve the name apostle" (1 Cor 15:9). He gloried only in the Lord (1 Cor 1:32), and in his own weaknesses, so that Christ's power might be made known (2 Cor 11:30; 12:5,9). The great and good qualities in Paul's nature remained intact, but they were ennobled. There still remained the powerful, unrelenting, moral zeal, but it had now become a determination to please God only in Jesus Christ, and to give greater glory to his Name. His passionate temperament had become transmuted into a burning love of Christ that ennobled his being, so that alongside his zeal for Christ's kingdom he retained a fervent and compassionate love for erring brethren. Paul had left far behind all self-assurance and pride, and from him shone out genuine divine *agape*, that was utterly selfless and sought only to be *agape*. Paul wanted to become a living and accurate revelation of the God of the New Testament, of the God who is *agape*, and who out of the *agape* with which he loves us, sent his beloved Son to suffer death in our world.

In this climate we are no longer dealing with cold law or severe morality. It is true that the moral law is not abrogated, but confirmed in the highest degree. Morality is no longer self-centered in aim; it serves the liberating *agape* of the Church of God. "When Christ freed us, he meant us to remain free" (Gal 5:1).

Neither the Church nor the human soul is any longer God's slave. "It is this that makes you a son, you are not a slave any more" (Gal 4:7). In God's beloved Son we have all become children of God, bearing his Spirit within us. It is not just a determination of will that makes us members of the God-man. We have through grace been given that membership by an inner physical bond; and through this bond with the God-man, who is the true Son of God, we have become united in grace to God himself. "You, God has made members of Christ Jesus and by God's doing he has become our wisdom, and our virtue, and our holiness, and our freedom" (1 Cor 1:30).

The Church or the individual soul has been transformed from slave into Bride of Christ. Paul sees tender conjugal love symbolized in the mystical marriage-bond between Christ and the Church. In freedom, bound only by *agape*, unconstrained by the fetters of the Law but united by the Spirit, the redeemed, liberated, sanctified and transfigured community, which is the Church or the individual soul, stands beside her Lord through whom she bears God himself within herself. From the Lord the Church receives into herself all life—his whole being. Here on earth she lives out this life in mystery, but one day that life will be unveiled and she will enjoy complete union of being for all eternity. The Church is one Spirit with him, and in his spiritual embrace enjoys eternal blessedness.

All his life long Paul suffered and fought for this view of the revelation proclaimed in the New Covenant. With superhuman effort he accomplished great things. His bitterest suffering was caused by fellow believers who did not understand him and who wanted to shackle Christianity in tight, human bonds.

Victoriously he fought on behalf of the Church of his beloved Christ for the *freedom of agape,* and by his accomplishment of this goal he became, as no other, a foundation of the Church. We give thanks to Christ for his apostle and hold faithfully to St Paul's exhortation: "Stand firm, therefore, and do not submit again to the yoke of slavery" (Gal 5:1).

Notes and References

For the most part the original text has been left as it stands. Occasional omissions and abbreviations concern, e.g., annotations added later by another hand, or lengthy quotations from scripture or the Fathers. References to liturgical texts not to be found in the revised liturgy have likewise been deleted.

Other references to liturgical texts have all been given and their present use in the liturgy (Eucharist or Divine Office) indicated. Casel has followed the numbering of the Psalms as in the Vulgate, the original text of which he has also used. For this reason no change has been made here. Notwithstanding earlier first publications, which in some cases are available, their publication in book-form has been taken as the norm for all texts, and to these sources reference is made below.

(For the English translation, references to liturgical texts has required further adjustment. In particular the Psalms have been numbered as in the Jerusalem Bible, although occasionally the text as in the Divine Office has been preferred.)

NOTES AND REFERENCES

1. Making Present the Mystery of Christ: *The meaning of the Christian Year*
From: *Das christliche Festmysterium*, Paderborn 194, 3-10.

(1) An ancient acclamation at the winter solstice: "The virgin has given birth, the light increases."

2. Advent: *The life-style of a Christian*
From: *Mysterium des Kommenden*, Paderborn 1952, 25-37.

(1) Clement of Alexandria, *Quis dives salvetur* 37.
(2) Clement of Alexandria, *Stromateis* VII 47, 4f.
(3) Clement of Alexandria, *Quis dives salvetur* 8, 2.

3. Christmas: *The Mystery of the Incarnation*
From: *Das christliche Festmysterium* 17-25.

(1) Song of the Trojan women, from Plutarch.
(2) From the *Bacchae* of Euripides.

4. Christmastide: *The crib and the cross*
From: *Mysterium des Kreuzes*, Paderborn 1954, 159-166.

(1) Ambrose, *Commentary on Luke* II 53.
(2) *Loc. cit.* 41.
(3) *Loc. cit,.*42f.
(4) *Loc. cit.* 44.

5. The Epiphany of our Lord: *Jesus, our way to God*
From: *Das christliche Festmysterium* 135-143.

(1) Celsus, quoted in Origen, *Against Celsus* VIII 12.
(2) *Ibid.*

6. Good Friday: *Authentic adoration of the cross*
From: *Mysterium des Kreuzes*, 196-203.

(1) Minusius Felix, *Octavius* 29, 6f.
(2) Hilary, *Tractatus on the Psalms*, Ps 118 Nun 9f., (CSEL) 22, 479f.
(3) *Loc. cit.* Ps 138: 29-31 (CSEL 22, 765f).

7. Easter: *The Lord's Pasch—passing over into new life*
From: *Das christliche Festmysterium*, 143-149.

(1) Gregory of Nazianzen, *Oratio* 45, 2.
(2) Leo the Great, *Sermons* 74, 2.

8. The Easter Season: *Pentecost—the symbol of completion*
From: *Das christliche Festmysterium*, 149-158.

9. The Ascension: *The glorified Christ with Cross in hand*
From: *Mysterium des Kreuzes*, 234-241.

(1) Versicle and Response on the feast of the Exaltation of the Cross.
(2) Introit on the feast of the Exaltation of the Cross.

10. Pentecost: *The Spirit—God gives himself to mankind*
From: *Das christliche Festmysterium*, 169-177.

11. The Assumption of Mary into heaven: *Abandonment to God is the way to life*
From: *Das christliche Festmysterium*, 199-206.

12. Peter and Paul: *The meaning of devotion to the saints*
From: *Das christliche Festmysterium*, 83-94.

(1) Clement of Alexandria, *Protreptikos* 59, 2f.
(2) "Dominus legem dat." An inscription on ancient Christian pictures, in which Christ is shown handing over a roll to Peter.

Literature

Casel, Odo: *Das christliche Kultmysterium*. Vierte durchgesehene und erweiterte Auflage herausgegeben von P. Burkhard Neunheuser OSB, Regensburg 1960.

–*Mysterientheologie. Ansatz und Gestalt*. Herausgegeben vom Abt-Herwegen-Institut der Abtei Maria Laach. Ausgewählt und eingeleitet von Arno Schilson, Regensburg 1986.

Fithaut, Theodor: *Die Kontroverse über die Mysterienlehre*, Warendorf 1947.

Krahe, Maria-Judith: "Der Herr ist der Geist." *Studien zur Theologie Odo Casels*. 1: Das Mysterium Christi. 2: Das Mysterium vom Pneuma Christi, St Ottilien 1986.

Neunheuser, Burkhard: Art. Casel, Odo, in *Theologische Realenzyklop*ädie 7 (1981) 643-647.

Schilson, Arno: *Theologie als Sakramententheologie. Die Mysterientheologie Odo Casels*, Mainz 1982.

Bibliographies

Santagada, Osvaldo D.: Dom Casel. Contributo monografico per una Bibliografica generale delle sue opere, degli studi sulla sua dottrina e della sua influenza nella teologia contemporanea, in *Archiv für Liturgiewissenschaft* 10 (1967) 7-77.

Häußling, Angelus A.: Bibliographie Odo Casel, OSB, 1967-1985. Mit einzelnen Nachträgen aus früheren Jahren, in: *Archiv für Liturgiewissenschaft* 28 (1986) 26-42.

Chronological table of Odo Casel's life and works

1886   27 September: Born in Koblenz

1905   Entered the Benedictine Abbey of Maria Laach

1911   Ordained priest in Rome

1912   Gained his doctorate in Rome with the thesis: "The Eucharistic Doctrine of St Justin Martyr"

1918   "The memorial of the Lord in early Christian liturgies. The basic concepts in the Canon of the Mass." In this Casel describes Jewish and pagan influences on the celebration of the Christian eucharist.

1919   Gained D.Phil at Bonn with De philosophorum Graecorum silentio mystico "On mystical silence in the Greek philosohers".

from 1921 Editor of the newly founded *Jahrbuch für Liturgiewissenschaft*.

1922   "Die Liturgie als Mysterienfeier." In this Casel expounds in detail the hermeneutic significance of the pagan mysteries for the Christian sacraments.

from 1922 Became spiritual director in the Convent of Benedictine Nuns at Herstelle (Weser).

1926   "Mysterium". A volume written in collaboration with other monks of Maria Laach, in which Casel expounds the central aspects of Mystery-theology. This initiated many-sided controversies which continued until his death.

1932   "Das christliche Kultmysterium." 4th edition 1960. This is a penetrating description of the shape of Mystery-theology, a kind of program.

1941   "Das christliche Festmysterium." An exposition of the Chrisian Year in the light of Mystery-theology.
"Glaube, Gnosis, Mysterium". A programmatic defense of the basic outlines of Mystery-theology, especially in respect of an insight into theology, cult, symbol and mystery.

1948   28 March (Easter morning). Odo Casel died in Herstelle.